LEGENDS OF WARFARE
NAVAL

USS Massachusetts (BB-59)
From World War II to Battleship Cove

DAVID DOYLE

Schiffer
Military History

4880 Lower Valley Road
Atglen, PA 19310

Designed by Alexa Harris
Cover design by Jack Chappell
Type set in Impact/Universe Lt Sd/Minion Pro
ISBN: 978-0-7643-6887-5
Printed in India

Published by Schiffer Publishing, Ltd.
4880 Lower Valley Road
Atglen, PA 19310
Phone: (610) 593-1777; Fax: (610) 593-2002
Email: Info@schifferbooks.com
Web: www.schifferbooks.com

For our complete selection of fine books on this and related subjects, please visit our website at www.schifferbooks.com. You may also write for a free catalog.

Schiffer Publishing's titles are available at special discounts for bulk purchases for sales promotions or premiums. Special editions, including personalized covers, corporate imprints, and excerpts, can be created in large quantities for special needs. For more information, contact the publisher.

We are always looking for people to write books on new and related subjects. If you have an idea for a book, please contact us at proposals@schifferbooks.com.

Acknowledgments

This book would not have been possible without the generous help of Chris Nardi of USS *Massachusetts* and my friends Tom Kailbourn, Tracy White, A. D. Baker III, and Scott Taylor. As always, my wonderful wife, Denise, took notes, scanned photographs, and accompanied me on some very hot days while photographing this storied vessel.

Unless otherwise noted, all archival photos are from the collections of the National Archives and Records Administration, and recent photos were taken by the author.

Times and dates given in the text are local times.

Contents

Introduction

USS *Massachusetts* (BB-59) was the fourth US Navy ship to be named for the commonwealth of Massachusetts. While BB-59 was one of the most successful battleships in US Navy history, her like-named predecessor, USS *Massachusetts* (BB-2), was not well regarded. BB-2, an Indiana-class battleship, was built in Philadelphia by William Cramp & Sons and was launched on June 10, 1893. She was commissioned exactly three years later. This ship, along with her sisters *Indiana* and *Oregon*, was intended for coastal defense work, with low range, low freeboard, and low displacement. She was armed with four 13-inch guns plus a secondary battery of eight 8-inch guns. The ship saw service in the Spanish-American War. Following an overhaul, in December 1898 she ran aground on Diamond Reef in New York Harbor, causing extensive damage requiring an immediate return to drydock for a further three months of repair.

In 1900 the ship was briefly placed in the reserve fleet, only to be reactivated a month later. In March 1901, she ran aground again, this time in Pensacola Harbor. In January 1903, a turret explosion killed nine of her crew, and in August she ran aground again off Maine, requiring a return to drydock. In December 1904, an engine room gasket failure killed three men and wounded several more. In January 1906, she was decommissioned and began a three-year modernization. She was recommissioned in May 1910 but, because of her age and obsolescence, was decommissioned yet again on May 23, 1914.

The need for ships and crews during World War I again brought her back into commission on June 9, 1917. Used for training, the ship was decommissioned a final time on March 31, 1919, having been renamed *Coast Battleship Number 2* on March 29.

Her name was stricken on November 22, 1920, and the ship was transferred to the War Department for use as a target by the Army by Fort Pickens in the Gulf of Mexico. She was sunk off Pensacola on January 6, 1921.

BB-2 had been renamed *Coast Battleship Number 2* in order to make the Massachusetts name available for BB-54, a unit of the proposed 1920 South Dakota (BB-49) class of 47,000-ton battleships. None of these ships were completed, with construction of *Massachusetts* having been suspended on February 8, 1922, owing to the restrictions of the 1922 Washington Naval Treaty. The ship was canceled on August 17, 1923, and the 11 percent completed hull of BB-54 was sold on November 8 of that year and scrapped on the builder's ways at Bethlehem Shipbuilding's Fore River Shipyard.

Thus, when a new generation of battleships was being planned, the name *Massachusetts* was still available.

Seen here early in her career, the first US battleship to carry the name of the commonwealth of Massachusetts was Battleship No. 2, this 10,288-ton Indiana-class battleship built by William Cramp & Sons' Ship and Engine Building Company in Philadelphia.

Massachusetts was repeatedly decommissioned and recommissioned and is shown here while laid up at Philadelphia Navy Yard in spring 1919. The laid-up battleships visible in this scene are, *left to right*, USS *Iowa* (BB-4), USS *Massachusetts* (BB-2), and USS *Indiana* (BB-1). The US Navy did not adopt the standard hull classification system until July 17, 1920, which was after she had been decommissioned the final time. Nevertheless, she and her contemporaries are often referred to by hull numbers under that system, as in "BB-2." *Naval History and Heritage Command*

Renamed Coast Battleship Number 2 on March 29, 1919, ex-*Massachusetts* was decommissioned the final time two days later. Subsequently, her hulk was loaned to the Army, which used her as a target off Pensacola, Florida, where she was sunk in 1921. Parts of her hulk remain visible today at low tide.

The planned 684-foot-long South Dakota–class battleships of 1920 were to be the most-powerful battleships of the US Navy of the time, boasting twelve 16"/50 guns in four triple turrets and a secondary armament of sixteen 6"/53 guns, with a displacement of 43,200 tons. The final unit of this planned class was to be BB-54, *Massachusetts*. Her keel was laid in Quincy on April 4, 1921. *Naval History and Heritage Command*

The incomplete hull of BB-54, USS *Massachusetts*, was photographed on the builder's ways on February 14, 1922, six days after work was stopped on her and twenty-one months before scrapping began.

CHAPTER 1
The Birth of a Battleship

USS *Massachusetts* (BB-59) and her three sister ships, *South Dakota* (BB-57), *Indiana* (BB-58*)*, and *Alabama* (BB-60*)*, together make up the next-to-the-last group of US Navy battleships—the South Dakota class. Among US battleships, only the Iowa-class battleships are newer. In March 1937, design work began on *Massachusetts* and the other South Dakota–class vessels—at the time, the yet-to-be-named ships were designated "Battleship 1939." The new design was so designated because it was slated for fiscal year 1939, which, in terms of the regular calendar, started on July 1, 1938. After approval was received on January 4, 1938, the characteristics would elicit congressional appropriation for two such battleships on April 4, 1938. These first two vessels—of the group destined to become the South Dakota class—were *South Dakota* (BB-57) and *Indiana* (BB-58). Tension around the world was escalating steadily, however. Japanese forces continued their rapid advance deep into China, having occupied the Chinese capital at the end of the previous year. Meanwhile in Europe, Germany's annexation of Austria in March 1938 led not to relaxation but to a new and greater crisis over Czechoslovakia, which dominated headlines that spring and summer. In light of such world developments, it is unsurprising that the US Congress moved to authorize construction of two more South Dakota–class battleships—*Massachusetts* (BB-59) and *Alabama* (BB-60)—on June 25, 1938.

The South Dakota ships were, like the North Carolina–class (*North Carolina* [BB-55] and *Washington* [BB-56]) ships before them, considered "treaty battleships." In the aftermath of World War I, there had been considerable international optimism about the prospect of avoiding another global war by limiting the size and effectiveness of warships. The major maritime powers were able to agree on a series of naval treaties that restricted ships' armament and size. In fact, the Washington Naval Treaty had caused the cancellation of Battleship (BB) 54, which was to have been named *Massachusetts*, on February 8, 1922. The keel for BB-54 had been laid at the Fore River Shipyard in April 1921, and the ship, which was about 11 percent complete, was broken up on the building ways in accordance with the treaty in late 1923. Battleships that conformed to the requirements of these naval treaties are often referred to as "treaty battleships."

These treaties restricted battleship displacement to 35,000 tons each and limited the warships' guns to a maximum 16-inch bore. It was the standard practice for a battleship's armor to be designed to protect it from an equally armed opponent. This meant, as far as the South Dakota–class battleships were concerned, that they would have sufficient armor to withstand gunfire from an enemy's 16-inch guns. To armor a battleship to that degree without exceeding the overall 35,000-ton displacement limit meant that the vessel had to be relatively short and compact. The weight limitation meant that the ship was not as well protected from torpedo attack as the designers would have liked. *Massachusetts'* length fell just under 680 feet, giving the ship a stubby configuration, the shape of its hull less than ideal hydrodynamically, as well as limiting the space available for machinery spaces. Because of these design characteristics imposed by the treaty limitations, *Massachusetts* had a top speed of 27.8 knots, or 32 miles per hour. The longer hull of the subsequent Iowa-class ships permitted more-powerful machinery, and thus a higher top speed, while retaining similar armament and improved protection.

All four South Dakota–class battleships were built at about the same time. New York Shipbuilding Company constructed *South Dakota*, Newport News Shipbuilding and Drydock Company produced *Indiana*, and the nearby Norfolk Navy Yard built *Alabama*, while *Massachusetts* was built by the Fore River Shipyard of the Bethlehem Steel Corporation in Quincy, Massachusetts, the same yard that had laid down BB-54.

She was launched on September 23, 1941, with Mrs. Frances Lovering Adams, wife of former secretary of the navy Charles Francis Adams III, as her sponsor. When a warship is launched, it is far from complete, and *Massachusetts* was no exception. The thousands of tons of steel that slid into the Weymouth Fore River was in essence only the basic structure of the formidable battleship to come. After launching, tugboats shoved the bulk of *Massachusetts*, herself incapable of moving at that time, to the shipyard's fitting-out pier. There, thousands of workmen continued to toil, erecting superstructure and installing weapons and electronic equipment, lockers, machinery, mess equipment, and the millions of other components big and small that are necessary to transform a great floating steel box into a functional warship.

As the ship was being fitted out, a crew was gathered. Ranks of experienced officers and enlisted men were stretched due to the war, which the nation had been involved in since the Japanese attack on Pearl Harbor, and thus 70 percent of *Massachusetts'* initial crew—known as "plank owners"—were draftees, and only 19 of her 113 officers had more than two years' service.

Following her seven-month fitting out, *Massachusetts* was delivered to the Boston Navy Yard in April 1942, where, on May 21, 1942, she was commissioned with Capt. Francis E. M. Whiting as her first captain.

Capt. Whiting addressed his crew during the commissioning ceremony, closing his remarks with

> They chose a motto for the seal of the Commonwealth of Massachusetts. It is a fighting motto—With the Sword It Seeks Peace Under Liberty.
>
> That is our motto, yours and mine. That is our assignment— To win peace under liberty, and to keep on fighting until we do win it. Our only purpose in life at this moment is battle; we must not waste a single hour in getting ready for it.
>
> I quoted a minute ago some American words that I like—"Damn the Torpedoes; Full Steam Ahead." I shall close with some famous

words that I do not like—"Don't Give Up the Ship." Those words were uttered by one of the bravest men who ever wore the uniform of the American Navy, your uniform and mine, Capt. James Lawrence. I honor him, but I resent the words because they were uttered at the end of a fight in which he and his men did not have a chance. They were the words of a dying captain, on a sinking ship, spoken to a brave but untrained crew. Because they were untrained, they were doomed.

So would we be doomed if we had to fight today even in this great ship, one of the biggest and most powerful in the world. We would be doomed because we are untrained. Our first business, our only business now, is to make this ship an efficient fighting unit, and to do it in the shortest possible time. We are going on a 24[-]hour basis.

I shall be intolerant of shirking. I intend to drive you because I am responsible for your lives. The quicker and better you are trained, the greater your chance for victory is, and the sooner we shall go home to an honorable peace. I shall give you full opportunity, but in the meanwhile "work" is our motto. I would not be doing my duty to you if I did not drive you and drive you hard.

The minute our training is complete, we shall show the world how the Massachusetts can take it and how she can dish it out. We shall prove that we appreciate the great traditions handed down to us. We shall be worthy of the name.

Officials have convened in the secretary of the navy's office on November 2, 1938, to open bids for the construction of three of the four battleships of the South Dakota class: *South Dakota* (BB-57), *Indiana* (BB-58), and *Massachusetts* (BB-59). Seated are, *left to right*, Adm. William D. Leahy, Chief of Naval Operations; Secretary of the Navy Claude Swanson; RAdm. Walter B. Woodson, Judge Advocate General; and RAdm. William G. DuBose, chief of the Bureau of Construction and Repair. Standing (*far right*) is RAdm. Harold G. Bowen, chief of the Bureau of Engineering. *Naval History and Heritage Command*

As of July 10, 1942, the ship was officially part of the Atlantic Fleet, and two days later she sailed for Casco Bay, Maine, beginning a seven-week period of active training, returning to the South Boston Navy Yard Annex on July 21 for inspection and additional yard work. The next day she was turned over to the commander of battleships, US Atlantic Fleet, and, on July 28, 1942, was reported as ready for shakedown cruises.

Massachusetts sailed from Boston on August 2, bound for Chesapeake Bay to begin a series of short training cruises, which began the next day. On August 17, 1942, she sailed again for Casco Bay, Maine, arriving the next day for further training exercises. This training continued until September 13, when she put into drydock at Navy Yard Boston for scheduled drydocking. She steamed for Chesapeake Bay, arriving at Hampton Roads on September 27. She anchored in Annapolis Roads for the first weekend of October, welcoming midshipmen aboard to see the Navy's newest battleship, then steamed to Casco Bay for machinery trials.

In August 1939, about a month into the construction of *Massachusetts*, work on the keel and the bottom of the hull had advanced from the bow (closest to the camera) to the amidships area. The bottom of most of the hull would have three skins, or layers of steel plate, which would contain a multitude of compartments: voids, containing only air, and spaces for fuel oil, fresh water, and reserve-feed water. The triple-bottom construction helped ensure the survivability of the ship in the event of torpedo strikes.

Construction of *Massachusetts* officially commenced with the laying of the keel on July 20, 1939, at the Bethlehem Shipbuilding Corporation's Fore River Shipyard, at Quincy, Massachusetts. Workers are guiding the placement of a keel plate onto wooden keel blocks. Subsequently, more plates and steel components would be riveted and welded together to form the keel, which served as the structural backbone of the hull.

The hull of *Massachusetts* is observed from the forward starboard quarter shortly before her launching, which took place on September 23, 1941. A wooden platform for the guests at the christening of the ship is in front of the bow. Above the ship are several of the Fore River Shipyard's double-runway lattice girder cranes, manufactured by Pawling & Harnischfeger.

Massachusetts is on the building ways at Fore River Shipyard soon before its launching. The hull has been painted gray, with a black boot topping—the wide stripe along the waterline, designed to mask the grease and oil that inevitably floats on the water in harbors and adheres to the hull. A large wooden cradle, called a poppet, is under the hull aft of the bow, and wooden props called shores help support the hull farther aft.

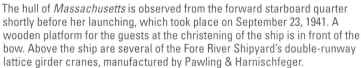

On launching day, September 23, 1941, workers are assembled below the stern of *Massachusetts*. Towering above them are the two huge rudders, each of which was about 273 square feet in size. Also in view are the propellers, all of which had four blades. The inboard propellers were 17 feet, 4.5 inches in diameter, while the outboard ones were 17 feet, 8 inches.

The lower part of the hull is viewed from below the port side of the quarterdeck, with the outboard port propeller and its shaft in the background. The wooden shores would have to be removed in a predetermined order prior to the launching of the ship.

The bottom of the starboard stern is viewed before the process to remove the shores begins, on launching day. The starboard outboard propeller is to the right of center.

All four propellers and the two rudders are in view in this photo taken from the aft port quarter. A series of shores are between each of the propellers. Lines are rigged to the tops of the shores to enable workers to lower them without damage to the ship or personnel.

On September 23, 1941, spectators and guests are assembled to witness the christening and the launching of *Massachusetts*. The forward starboard part of the hull is to the right, with several heaps of drag chains in center. These chains were attached to the hull, and as the hull slid down the ways upon launching, the drag of the chains acted to control the momentum of the ship. *Naval History and Heritage Command*

Naval and civilian officials are on the christening platform shortly before the launching of the ship. The shape of the bulbous bow is depicted clearly. This feature was designed to increase fuel efficiency, speed, and stability by reshaping the way that water flowed around the hull. Ready for launching at Quincy, Massachusetts, September 23, 1941. In the background are piles of drag chains and a sign attached to the keel for the light cruiser *Flint* (CL-64; later renamed USS *Vincennes*), which would be laid down here after the launching of *Massachusetts*. *Naval History and Heritage Command*

Frances Lovering Adams, seen with her husband, former Secretary of the Navy Charles Francis Adams III, was the sponsor of the battleship *Massachusetts*. Immediately before the launching of the ship, she broke the ceremonial bottle of champagne on the bow, a traditional component of a ship's christening and launching ceremony. *Naval History and Heritage Command*

Part of the crowd attending the launching of *Massachusetts* is seen from the temporary wooden tower erected for cameramen to the front of the bow. The ship was out of view to the right. This view was taken well before the launching, since numerous spectators are standing on and next to the heaps of drag chains. *Naval History and Heritage Command*

A photographer captured the moment Frances Adams dashed the ceremonial bottle of champagne against the side of the bow of *Massachusetts*, directly below white draft marks aligned vertically on the bow. These numerical marks indicated the distance between the waterline and the bottom of the hull.

Bunting on the bow of *Massachusetts* billows out as the just-launched ship slides into the water at the Fore River Shipyard. No sooner had the battleship cleared the ways than workers, with the assistance of a gantry crane, moved a section of the keel for the cruiser Flint into place (*lower left*) so assembly of that ship could commence on these building ways. *Naval History and Heritage Command*

Following the launching of *Massachusetts*, tugboats are maneuvering the ship into position alongside an outfitting dock at Bethlehem's Fore River Shipyard on September 23, 1941. Here, the ship would be completed. Construction of the superstructure was already underway, and conical awnings had been erected over the openings of the barbettes, upon which the 16-inch gun turrets would eventually be mounted.

A little over two weeks after her launching, *Massachusetts* is moored to the outfitting dock (*left*) at Fore River on October 8, 1941. Work on the conning tower had advanced since the launching; it is at the front of the superstructure. Nested to the port side of Massachusetts are the tanker *Sinclair Superflame* and the light cruisers *San Diego* (CL-53) and *San Juan* (CL-54). After the completion of the ship's fitting out, she was commissioned into the service of the US Navy on May 12, 1942.

This photo and the following sequence of images were taken during USS *Massachusetts'* passage from the Fore River Shipyard, in Quincy, to the South Boston Navy Yard Annex on May 12, 1942, where on that day the battleship was delivered to the US Navy and commissioned into the service. This was the beginning of the battleship's first shakedown cruise, from Boston to Casco Bay, Maine. Construction of the ship was substantially complete, but she still lacked items such as air-search, surface-search, and fire-control radar antennas and blast bags for 16-inch and 5-inch guns.

Massachusetts is viewed from off her port bow. In accordance with a November 1941 order, the ship was painted in a modified Measure 12 camouflage with irregular splotches replacing the normal Measure 12 straight, graded lines. The scheme combined Navy Blue (5-N) and Ocean Gray (5-O) patterns on the hull and the first level of the superstructure, and Ocean Gray and Haze Gray (5-H) on the remainder of the superstructure.

Tugboats are gathering around USS *Massachusetts* as she enters Boston Harbor. Much of the boot topping is showing above the surface of the water. Once the ship was fully provisioned and outfitted, much less of the boot topping would be visible. At least one author has claimed that military censors "removed" all radar antennas from the May 1942 photos of *Massachusetts*, but a careful examination of this series leads to the conclusion that no radar antennas were present, although support frames for the fire-control radar antennas on the secondary-battery directors had been installed.

This aerial photo of the battleship was taken a moment after the preceding one. Faintly visible is the gallery of three 20 mm antiaircraft guns on the rear of the roof of turret 2; these were positioned inside an elongated splinter shield. These photos reveal that flat, temporary structures were on the tops of the turrets: possibly temporary covers or platforms.

In an aerial photograph of *Massachusetts* from approximately 400 feet above her starboard stern, the battleship enters Boston Harbor on May 12, 1942. At the upper left and center are buoys supporting a harbor-defense net; at the top center is a net tender. The temporary structures on the turret tops, which jutted slightly beyond the fronts and sides of the turrets, are particularly evident in this view. Notably, despite plans to install six 1.1" quad antiaircraft guns aboard *Massachusetts*, as can be seen here, the large tubs have neither the 1.1" nor the later 40 mm quad mounts installed as of this date. *Naval History and Heritage Command*

Six tugboats have come alongside *Massachusetts* to assist her in her passage of Boston Harbor on May 12, 1942. Visible on the stern is the aircraft crane, to the sides of which are the two aircraft catapults, for launching gunnery-spotting floatplanes.

Members of the commissioning crew of *Massachusetts* are in evidence on the decks and bridges during the battleship's May 12, 1942, transit of Boston Harbor. Towering above the superstructure is the fire-control tower, which rose six levels above the top of the pilothouse (which occupied the second-from-the-top level of the conning tower, at the front of the superstructure). At the top of the tower is the forward Mk. 38 director, which tracked surface targets and transmitted those data to the fire-control system, where firing solutions were computed for the 16-inch/45-caliber gun batteries. While the ship was in the Boston Navy Yard in the coming weeks, Mk. 8 fire-control radar antennas would be mounted atop the ship's two Mk. 38 directors.

The light- and dark-colored temporary panels on the tops of all three 16-inch/45-caliber gun turrets are prominent in this final photo of *Massachusetts* in Boston Harbor on May 12, 1942. Soon, the ship would receive further outfitting and provisioning to prepare her for combat operations.

In a view from the starboard of *Massachusetts* under steam in Boston Harbor, the tubes of the 16-inch/45-caliber guns of turret 1 (the forward turret) are painted in a wavy camouflage pattern, with a dark color on top and a lighter gray on the bottom. The 16-inch tubes of turrets 2 and 3 are painted a light gray, with the camouflage pattern to be applied later. *Naval History and Heritage Command*

On July 12, 1942, USS *Massachusetts* put out to sea for the first time, on a shakedown cruise to Casco Bay, Maine. As seen in a photograph taken on the following day, blast bags had been installed on the 16-inch and 5-inch guns, to seal off the spaces between the gun shields and the gun barrels. Recently the foremast had been installed to the rear of the forward fire-control tower and radar antennas had been mounted on the Mk. 37 and Mk. 38 gun fire directors. On the catapults are two Vought OS2U Kingfisher observation floatplanes, used for gunnery spotting, antisubmarine patrolling, rescue, and other purposes.

The newly installed foremast, as viewed from the starboard side in a photo taken July 13, 1942, was much higher than the mainmast, located aft of the smokestack. An SC-1 air-search radar antenna was on top of the foremast. Just aft of the mainmast is the aft fire-control tower, atop which is the aft Mk. 38 main-battery director. Both of the main-battery directors were now fitted with Mk. 3 fire-control radar antennas. The four Mk. 37 secondary-battery directors, which controlled the 5-inch/38-caliber gun mounts, now were equipped with Mk. 4 radar antennas. The forward Mk. 37 director is between the top of the conning tower and the forward fire-control tower.

USS *Massachusetts* is making a speed run on a calm sea on July 13, 1942. Turrets 1 and 2 are trained in opposite directions, while turret 3 is trained to port. Life rafts are stored on the tops and sides of all three turrets. *Naval History and Heritage Command*

CHAPTER 2
To War in the Atlantic

Returning to Boston on October 16, *Massachusetts* took aboard ammunition and stores and topped off her fuel bunkers, making ready to put to sea. Loaded, she anchored in Casco Bay on October 20 and the next day took aboard RAdm. Robert C. Giffen and his staff, becoming the flagship of the just-formed Task Group (TG) 34.1, the covering group for an amphibious assault force formed to land in French North Africa, the first offensive operation by the US in the European/African theater of operations.

Massachusetts weighed anchor on a rainy Sunday, October 25, and, joining with Cruiser Division 7, USS *Tuscaloosa* (CA-37) and *Wichita* (CA-45), and escorting ships of Destroyer Division 8, USS *Wainwright* (DD-419), *Jenkins* (DD-407), *Rhind* (DD-404), and *Mayrant* (DD-402), steamed toward Hampton Roads. There the fighting ships joined with the transports, which were Task Group 34.8. Together, Task Groups 34.1 and 34.8, along with Carrier Group 34.2 and a second amphibious force, TG 34.9, composed Task Force 34 (in all, 102 ships), under the command of RAdm. H. Kent Hewitt.

After steaming across the Atlantic, sometimes in rough seas (during which *Massachusetts'* third Kingfisher spotting plane was destroyed by water breaking over the deck on November 4, 1942), as the Task Force neared North Africa at 1415 on November 6, Capt. Whiting manned the loudspeaker and read to this message from Adm. Giffen to the officers and men:

The time has now come to prove ourselves worthy of the trust placed in us by our nation. If circumstances force us to fire upon the French, once our victorious ally, let it be done with the firm conviction that we are striking not at the French people, but at the men who prefer Hitler's slavery to freedom. If we fight, hit hard and break clean. There is glory enough for us all. Good luck. Go with God.

Capt. Whiting immediately followed this with his own message:

As commanding officer of the Massachusetts, I wish to add the following: We commissioned the Massachusetts only six months ago; never have I seen a more responsive and hardworking ship's

company than this one. You have met every demand I have made. We have the finest ship's spirit possible. We are ready. If it becomes our duty to open fire tomorrow, never forget the motto of the commonwealth of Massachusetts, whose name we proudly bear. That motto is "With the Sword She Seeks Peace Under Liberty." If we wield the sword, do so with all the strength in this mighty ship to destroy completely and quickly.

The war diary of Cruiser Division Seven, *Massachusetts*, flagship, noted that "during the evening run toward our objective[,] mass was celebrated in one of the crew compartments of the ship and there was a large attendance. Later general services were held."

The next day, November 7, at 0700, Adm. Hewitt signaled, "Proceed on service assigned." With that, the cover force, Task Group 34.1, including *Massachusetts*, steamed toward Casablanca, intent on containing the French fleet in the harbor there, thus protecting the US Army 3rd Division, which would be landing 12 miles northeast at Felda. It had been hoped that the landings would be peaceful, since many French in North Africa were loyal to the Allies, and the copy was that the Vichy French would defect to the Free French.

On November 8, *Massachusetts'* crew had an early breakfast at 0400, then manned their battle stations. At 0618, *Massachusetts* launched one of her Vought OS2U-3 Kingfisher spotting aircraft, with a second being launched two minutes later (her third had been lost to heavy seas on the voyage from the US), and *Wichita* and *Tuscaloosa* launched their own spotting aircraft, Curtiss SOC Seagulls, at about the same time. At 0642, USS *Massachusetts* and other ships in the covering force received the signal "Play Ball"—the order to commence the attack.

The big ships steamed a trapezoidal pattern 20,000–28,000 yards from Casablanca to seal the harbor.

While this was happening, Vichy French pilots flying Curtiss H75A-1 fighters, an export version of the P-36A Hawk, shot down *Massachusetts'* Kingfisher Bureau Number (BuNo) 5804, flown by Ens. Thomas Doherty, with ARM2C Robert Etheridge in the back seat. The Kingfisher made a crash landing off shore, and the men were taken prisoner.

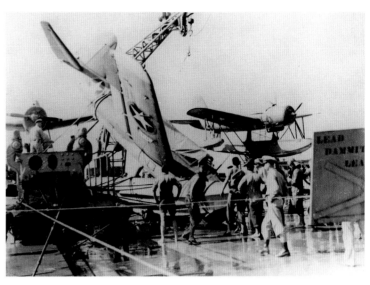

Following her seven-week shakedown cruise to Casco Bay and a subsequent period of posttrial inspections and outfitting in Boston and Norfolk, Virginia, USS *Massachusetts* returned to Casco Bay, from which she departed on October 24, 1942, bound for North Africa with Task Group 34.1. It was serving as the flagship of RAdm. Robert C. Giffen. During the Atlantic crossing, on November 4, a large wave crashed into the fantail, severely damaging one of the ship's Vought OS2U Kingfisher observation floatplanes, which was lashed to the deck. This event left only two of the ship's three Kingfishers available for duty.

The wave that struck the Kingfisher tore off the wing floats and broke the pylons that attached the center float to the belly of the fuselage. The two surviving Kingfishers are secured to the catapults. To the right is the shield of a 20 mm antiaircraft gun, on which is stenciled "LEAD DAMMIT LEAD," an injunction to the gunner to properly lead aerial targets to compensate for their trajectory.

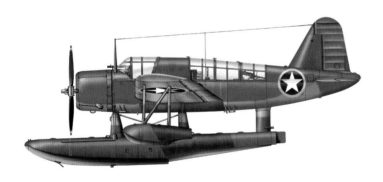

USS *Massachusetts* carried a number of different OS2U-1 and OS2U-3 scouting planes during her career. The initial complement was three aircraft, with one stowed on each of the two catapults and the third stowed on the deck between them. However, the number of aircraft assigned was sometimes less. They were launched via the catapults and recovered by landing in the sea, being hoisted aboard by the stern crane. This particular aircraft was carried during her Atlantic deployment.

A few minutes later, at 0659, the other Kingfisher, BuNo 5805, flown by Lt. Cmdr. Doerflinger, radioed, "Am coming in on starboard bow with a couple of hostile aircraft on my tail. Pick them off—I am the one in front." When the Kingfisher appeared overhead, *Massachusetts*' mounts 1 and 3 opened fire on the pursuing aircraft under the control of director 1, expending thirty-five rounds and forcing the French away.

At 0700 the French shore battery El Hank as well as the incomplete French battleship *Jean Bart* opened fire on the American fleet, dispelling hope of a peaceful landing.

Although planned to be formidable, *Jean Bart* was incomplete: only one of her main battery turrets, containing four 15-inch guns, was installed, and only a partial antiaircraft battery was aboard. Only a portion of her machinery had been made operational when she fled her builders' yard at Saint-Nazaire, and a blade of one her screws, only two of which had been installed in France, had been damaged in a grounding during her departure from France on June 19, a desperate effort to keep the ship from coming under Nazi control.

At Casablanca, she was moored at Quai Delinde, just around the corner from where the French liner *Porthos* was docked. The liner had arrived the evening before laden with civilians, including many women and children, who had fled Dakar. Fortunately, most of the people aboard *Porthos* had begun disembarking at 0545.

The shore battery El Hank, just south of Casablanca, opened fire on *Massachusetts* with 7.64-inch guns, firing four salvos, the first of which straddled the ship. *Wichita* took El Hank under fire, while *Massachusetts* turned 40 degrees and at 0703 opened fire on *Jean Bart* at a range of 24,400 yards—firing the first 16-inch shells of the war. *Massachusetts'* war diary noted, "Target—JEAN BART. Director fire, indirect following stable vertical and range keeper using a basic bearing that had been obtained on El Hand lighthouse. Fire nine salvos of from six to nine shots, each. Plane spot was used when fall of shot was observed. Enemy smoke screens and haze obscured the target. At least one hit on target and two on Mole du Commerce was reported during this period. Radars were inoperative during these salvos."

Three minutes later, *Jean Bart* returned fire with a two-gun salvo, her rounds missing *Massachusetts* by 600 yards; three minutes later, the French gunners' aim had improved, with those rounds falling close to port of the American battleship.

Massachusetts noted at 0717, "Divided fire of main battery. Checked fire with Turret 3. Continued firing on JEAN BART with Turrets 1 and 2. Fired thirteen salvos of from three to six shots each. At this point the navigation range was 23,700 yards."

At 0720, it was recorded, "Commenced firing with Turret 3 on the shore batteries on El Hank Point. Target—four shore batteries on El Hank Point, director fire. Fired five salvos from one to three guns each. Plane spot was used when fall of shot was observed. These batteries were temporarily silenced. The navigational range to El Hank was 22,900 yards on bearing 173 degrees (T). The range then increased to 30,400 yards at 0740."

Aboard and nearby *Jean Bart*, considerable punishment was being recorded. At 0725, one of *Massachusetts'* 16-inch armor-piercing rounds came crashing down on the French ship's deck, passing through both armored decks and exploding in the 152 mm magazines, which, fortunately for those on the receiving end, were empty since the guns had not yet been installed, thus preventing catastrophic damage to the Vichy battleship.

Massachusetts inflicted more havoc on the French battleship starting at 0735, when the first of four rounds in as many minutes took their toll. First, a round hit near the bow, the concussion deforming the hull plating; one minute later, another struck the mooring quay, showering the *Jean Bart* with concrete fragments, not only injuring antiaircraft crews but further piercing the hull and adding to the flooding. A third round punched through the ship's funnel, angling down and exiting at the armored deck. The fourth round hit the edge of the quay, then ricocheted through

On November 4, 1942, four days before beginning offensive operations off Casablanca, crewmen in the 20 mm gun battery on top of turret 2 of USS *Massachusetts* observe ships of Task Force 34 passing by in the Atlantic, including the battleship USS *Texas* (BB-35 in the left distance). Faintly visible on both armored shields of the 20 mm gun in the foreground is stenciled "LEAD DAMMIT LEAD." These stencils are visible on other 20 mm gun mounts in photos of this battleship, suggesting that they very possibly were on all the 20 mm mounts.

the outer plating, striking the armor belt, which deflected the round downward through the bottom of the ship. The round did not explode owing to a defective fuse, which dated to 1918.

Jean Bart and El Hank were not the only recipients of *Massachusetts'* firepower. A French destroyer flotilla was tied up nearby, and scattered about the harbor were other military and civilian ships.

At 0736, one of *Massachusetts'* 16-inch rounds hit the liner *Porthos*, moored near *Jean Bart*. Lacking armor, the French liner quickly capsized, taking twenty-four people with her. At 0755, a pair of the battleship's rounds hit the tanker *Ile d'Ouessant*, sinking her. The freighter *Ile de Noirmoutier* had the misfortune of being tied up immediately behind *Jean Bart*, and at 0810 she was hit by a 16-inch round, causing major flooding. Tied up behind *Ile de Noirmoutier* was the screw steamer *Fauzon*, which was hit twice, once at 0800 and again 0815, but remarkably the ship stayed afloat.

At 0806, a 16-inch round landed near the large French destroyer *Le Malin*, with shell splinters riddling the ship, killing seven while the shell cap ripped an 80-foot hole in the ship, flooding her boiler and forward engine rooms and causing her to settle and list to port.

At the same time *Le Malin* was hit, *Jean Bart* took a 16-inch round near the front of her only operational main battery turret. *Massachusetts'* shell pushed the French glacis plate down, jamming the turret.

Moments later, a second round hit the barbette for the absent number 2 turret and broke up rather than detonating. Splinters from this round ricocheted off the armored deck and penetrated several compartments, causing minor damage. At 0810, *Massachusetts* hit *Jean Bart* for the last time, this round landing on the quarterdeck just forward of the starboard catapult, penetrated the armor deck, and exploded in a ballast compartment, with fragments piercing the hull, causing additional flooding that overtook the steering compartment.

While some volumes state that *Massachusetts* sank *Jean Bart*, in fact the French ship, though it did take on water, continued in the fight until an armistice was signed with the French forces in Morocco on November 11. Her sole main battery turret was brought back into operation by 1724 and on November 10 was used to fire upon the flagship USS *Augusta*, after which carrier aircraft attacked the French vessel.

However, *Massachusetts* had kept the French ship in check for forty-eight hours and wreaked further damage in the port, as we have seen. But her battle off North Africa did not end with the crippling of the *Jean Bart*.

RAdm. Giffen ordered a ceasefire at 0835, with *Massachusetts'* war diary noting, "The Admiral has received word from the beach that the army is receiving no resistance and that the navy is killing the townspeople."

The source of the message that Adm. Giffen received is unknown, and the ceasefire was short lived, since in fact the Vichy were still engaged. However, the ceasefire order from the admiral came at an opportune time for the men of *Massachusetts'* turret 3, where at 0812 a shell had, during parbuckling (the process used to move a round from storage onto the turret turntable), tipped and caught in the hoist, jamming the turret. Clearing the jam of a 2,700-pound shell is a laborious task, yet the men were able to do this in only thirty-five minutes.

Ironically, at the same time that turret 3 went out of action due to the parbuckling issue, so did turret 1, although that turret was cleared in about five minutes. Both these incidents were attributed to fatigue on the part of the crew, which compounded problems that had been discovered in alignment, the latter later corrected.

As the men were clearing the round, some of the French ships sortied, with French light cruiser *Primauguet*, two destroyer leaders, and four fleet destroyers escaping the harbor, steaming toward the invasion fleet, thirty minutes away off Fedala. The sailing of two French submarines two minutes later was reported to Adm. Giffen, but the departure of the surface ships apparently went unreported—thus Task Group 34.1, the covering force, apparently failed in its objective to contain the Vichy fleet in Casablanca Harbor.

The approaching French vessels were spotted by Wildcats providing air support to the Fedala invasion force. The American aviators dove in, strafing the ships, while at the same time radioing the presence of the intruders to the US fleet. At 0825 the French ships opened fire on three US destroyers escorting the invasion force. Moments later, the flagship of the invasion force, Hewitt's *Augusta*, shifted her mission from shore bombardment to surface action and was soon joined in this by *Brooklyn* (CL-40). The French were routed, but not before sinking one landing craft and damaging several others.

At 0845, Adm. Hewitt radioed Adm. Giffen, ordering him to cover the transports off Fedala. Almost simultaneously, Giffen, who had received reports of two destroyers leaving Casablanca Harbor, had radioed Hewitt, asking if he needed assistance. Ultimately, at 0855 Capt. Whiting ordered *Massachusetts* to swing to 108 degrees (T) and proceed at 27 knots toward Fedala. At 0914, *Massachusetts* received from Adm. Hewitt this message: "Destroy enemy cruisers between Casablanca and Fedala. Report when in contact."

Following the Atlantic crossing, *Massachusetts* commenced its mission to support the Allied landings at Casablanca, French Morocco, on the morning of November 8, 1942. That strategically important port was occupied by Vichy French forces, aligned with the Axis powers, and their assets included a battleship, *Jean Bart*, which, although docked in the port, was nonetheless a lethal threat, with its main battery of four 15-inch guns (only one of its two four-gun turrets was operational). Here, *Massachusetts* is underway off Casablanca on November 8, as photographed from the destroyer USS *Mayrant* (DD-402). During this battle, *Massachusetts* flew two large national ensigns from the masts.

At 0916 the men of *Massachusetts* spotted the French ships off the starboard bow, making heavy smoke. Two minutes later she opened fire, at a range of 19,400 yards. Her war diary noted: "Targets—six enemy ships, DLs and DDs. Visibility reduced by haze and smoke. Fired thirty-five salvos of from three to nine shots each."

Forced to rely on optical spotting because of repeated electrical failures of her radars, *Massachusetts* shifted targets frequently, engaging the various French destroyers as well as the French cruiser *Pimauguet* as they became visible through the smoke and haze.

By 0935, *Massachusetts*' range had closed to 11,500 yards, very nearly point-blank range for the big rifles of the battleship, when suddenly she swung about. Regarding this maneuver, the ship's log notes only that this was done to prevent her from steaming into "restricted waters."

At 0940, one of the 16-inch rounds found its mark on *Fougueux*, a 2,000-ton destroyer, sinking the Vichy ship.

Massachusetts' war diary noted that three minutes later, "enemy shells were falling within fifty yards of the ship on both sides," and, two minutes after that, that "shell fragments were falling close aboard." After losing sight of those firing on her due to smoke, at 0953 she resumed replying to the French gunfire,

and three minutes after resuming fire, another 16-round found its mark, hitting the *Milan* from a range of 28,000 yards, mortally wounding the Vichy vessel.

Massachusetts, now steaming away from Fedala and back toward Casablanca, once again came within range of El Hank, and this time it was the French gunners who found their mark, also at 28,000 yards, with a 194 mm (7.3 inch) round penetrating the portside main deck, abreast turret 2. The round detonated against the armored second deck, exploding in the Marines' compartment and damaging bunks, lockers, and gear but inflicting no injuries to personnel.

Unknown to her crew at the time, *Massachusetts* was also being targeted by the submarine *Méduse*, whose spread of four torpedoes fired from only 800 yards were sighted running toward the battleship at 1003. Quick work at the helm turned the massive battlewagon such that torpedoes 3 and 4 passed parallel to her flanks, although one was within 15 feet of her hull, a narrow margin indeed.

Her war diary notes that at 1016, *Massachusetts* broke off action. By this time the ship had expended large amounts of her 16-inch armor-piercing shells (there were no high-capacity rounds aboard), and Adm. Hewitt was concerned that the French would

The Vought OS2U Kingfisher on the port catapult of *Massachusetts* has a cover installed over the front of the radial engine during operations in support of the Casablanca landings. A depth bomb is shackled to the underwing pylon for use against enemy submarines.

dispatch the battleship *Richelieu*, in port 1,500 miles away, to disrupt the landing, and he thus wanted to conserve ammunition.

The pause in firing was brief, however, since at 1030 she opened fire on the French 2nd Light Squadron at sea, and five minutes later the main battery went into rapid fire, with her gunners claiming four hits on the *Boulonnais*. At 1050, *Massachusetts* again came under fire, with the French rounds growing ever closer, finally making contact at 1057. At that time, a 155 mm round bounced off the battleship's starboard quarter and burst above 20 mm group 13, starting a small fire. No one was injured, since the men assigned to those guns had previously been moved to the unengaged side of the ship.

At 1101, mounts 1, 3, 5, 7, and 9 of *Massachusetts'* secondary battery opened fire on automatic, shelling a French destroyer with 105 5-inch rounds by the time firing ceased at 1103. Two minutes later, secondary firing resumed as *Massachusetts* changed course to recover Doerflinger's Kingfisher, which had landed, out of gas. The 5-inch mounts expended a further seventy-seven rounds. Doerflinger's Kingfisher was back aboard at 1130.

Giffen radioed Hewitt at 1245, saying, "Flagship has 53 16" projectiles and charges per gun remaining while WICHITA and TUSCALOOSA have 20 percent of their allowance main armament remaining. Shall I retain 16" for probable sortie of RICHELIEU or reduce El Hank."

At 1336, *Massachusetts'* only remaining Kingfisher was back in the air, now piloted by Ens. J. A. Cotton; four minutes later, the main battery fired two salvos at a French destroyer, and one minute later, El Hank answered in support of the targeted ship.

At 1340, Adm. Hewitt radioed Adm. Giffen again, urging that he concentrate on the French fleet, saying, "Light Forces Casablanca making reported sorties. Destroy them before nightfall."

At 1345, *Massachusetts* fired seven nine-gun salvos at El Hank. That the French battery continued to fire is indicative of the unsuitability of armor-piercing ammunition for engagement of such targets, but armor piercing was the only type of ammunition that had been loaded on *Massachusetts* before the ship had steamed from the US. In fact, Adm. Giffen had asked Adm. Hewitt to dispatch carrier-based bombers to attack El Hank with high-explosive bombs.

Finally, at 1423, Adm. Hewitt responded to Giffen's earlier question, radioing, "Your 1245 retain for possible sortie of RICHELIEU."

During the early-morning part of the Battle of Casablanca on November 8, 1942, crewmen on the afterdeck of *Massachusetts* observe as flak bursts blossom above a US ship in the background. This fire was an effort to drive off Vichy French aircraft that were menacing the task group. To the left is the forward part of the port catapult. At the center is a 20 mm gun mount; at least ten ammo magazines for the gun are lined up on the deck. *Naval History and Heritage Command*

A shell from *Jean Bart* sends up a plume of water as it plunges into the ocean near the wake of USS *Massachusetts*.

As *Massachusetts'* big guns dueled with the Vichy French battleship *Jean Bart*, moored in the port of Casablanca, a photographer aboard *Massachusetts* captured an image of a shell from the *Jean Bart* as it splashed into the water near the ship. *Naval History and Heritage Command*

RAdm. Robert C. Giffen, USN, views the Battle of Casablanca from the bridge of his flagship, USS *Massachusetts.* A 1907 graduate of the US Naval Academy, Giffen was a destroyer captain in World War I.

RAdm. Robert C. Giffen, center, looks up at the photographer during a lull in the Battle of Casablanca. To the left, on the 20 mm gun shield, is stenciled the ubiquitous "LEAD DAMMIT LEAD." *Naval History and Heritage Command*

Two national ensigns flew from USS *Massachusetts* during the Casablanca battle. Above them is the flag of RAdm. Robert C. Giffen, commander of the naval force that was covering the landings near Casablanca. *Naval History and Heritage Command*

Massachusetts' guns remained silent until 1558, when the decision was made to unload the guns through the muzzles. Turret 2 fired a ranging salvo at El Hank, 30,300 yards away. This was followed by a six-gun salvo from turrets 1 and 3. As it turned out, this was the best shot of the day against the French battery, with the war diary of the commander of Task Group 34.1 recording, "When our last three-gun salvo landed[,] there could be seen a blinding flash ashore, and it was reported that we had demolished the military stores on the beach."

At 1605, *Massachusetts* secured from general quarters, her exhausted crew having fired 786 16-inch rounds, the record for any ship in any engagement of the war. Only forty-one rounds per gun remained in her magazines.

During the night of November 12, its mission complete, Task Group 34.1 was ordered to return to the United States, with *Massachusetts* to tie up in Boston, much to the pleasure of its crew. However, those orders were changed on November 14, which instead ordered TG 34.1 to Norfolk. The war diary of the commander of Task Group 34.1 noted, "To the delight of all hands, a course was laid out that would bring us to Boston, but a dispatch from Cinclant thre[w] cold water on the enthusiasm. We have been ordered to Norfolk, VA, (What a lousy place) there to load ammunition and stores. . . . Much of the joy has gone out of life for some who feel Norfolk offers less than the inhospitable shores of French Morocco."

As the task group steamed through squalls, the men of USS *Massachusetts* prepared to refuel escort ships, whose hungry boilers were indifferent to the weather. The Task Group 34.1 war diary noted on Sunday, November 15, "Church services were held aboard the USS *Massachusetts*, Flagship of Task Group 34.1 were well attended today. The Casablanca action with those near misses from the *Jean Bart* and shore batteries at El Hank certainly has made a lot of Christians out of these sailors."

The task group war diary recorded on November 19 that "when the ships reach Norfolk, the *Massachusetts* and *Tuscaloosa* will load ammunition and then proceed to the Navy Yard, Boston[,] for 10 days['] availability [the navy term for shipyard repairs]."

Massachusetts' war diary for November 20, 1942, noted: "At 0910 sighted buoy #1 marking entrance to swept channel to mouth of Chesapeake Bay. Units of group steamed into Norfolk, VA. Independently. Sighted USS *Alabama* and escorting destroyers shortly after daylight. Land sighted at 1126. Test firing of 20 mm and 40 mm machine guns held in morning. At 1647 ship moored port side to Pier #7, berth Queen, Naval Operating Base, Norfolk, VA., having completed duty as Commander Task Force 34.1 (operation plan 1-42.)"

The next day, Adm. Giffen transferred his flag to *Wichita* (CA-45), and *Massachusetts* began taking on ammunition and powder charges, and that process would continue through November 23. During that time, she also took aboard 278,082 gallons of fuel oil.

On November 25, she departed for Boston, tying up at the West Jetty, Navy Yard Annex, South Boston, at 1445 the next day;

the ship's record noted, "Navy Yard began alterations and repairs to the ship immediately." This work would continue through December 10.

Her log for December 11 notes, "At 1025 underway from alongside West Jetty South Boston Navy Yard. . . . Ship's draft prior to getting underway 35' 1" forward and 34' 11" aft." At 1630 that day, she dropped anchor in Berth V-5 in Casco Bay, Maine, where, but for short trips for gunnery training, she remained until Christmas Eve, when she steamed back to the Boston Navy Yard Annex. On December 29, she moved into the Navy Yard for availability to complete the previously begun repairs and alterations.

The next day, *Massachusetts* again steamed to Casco Bay, where she remained until Saturday, February 6, 1943. The log entry for that day notes, "1158 underway from Berth Able-3, Casco Bay, Portland, Main, en route Colon, Panama Canal Zone, in company with USS *Philips*, USS *Eaton* and USS *Renshaw*." The next day, the small fleet of ships encountered heavy seas, which tore equipment lose on the forecastle and caused flooding of the main switchboard through ventilation ducts.

On February 11, *Massachusetts* entered the swept channel to Cristóbal, Colón, Canal Zone, tying up at Pier 8 at 1650, where she remained until 0606 the next day. At 1210 on February 13, while clearing the Pedro Miguel Locks, the starboard propeller caught on the lock safety chain. At 1553 she tied up at Pier 18, Balboa, where the Canal Zone repair force made emergency repairs, in part due to the heavy weather encountered on February 7. Repairs complete, on February 15 she steamed for the South Pacific.

Crewmen go about their business on the afterdeck of *Massachusetts* during a lull in the Battle of Casablanca. In the right foreground, to the rear of turret 3, is a plenum chamber. To the far right is the top of the aircraft catapult, which is lowered in its stowed position. *Naval History and Heritage Command*

The Vichy French battleship *Jean Bart* was the principal opponent of USS *Massachusetts* in the Battle of Casablanca. Laid down in 1936, the uncompleted ship was hustled out of France for Casablanca to keep her out of German possession at the time of the fall of France in 1940. Although unable to sally out from the harbor during the battle, *Jean Bart* posed a significant threat with her four 15-inch guns. This aerial photo of the battleship was taken from an aircraft from the carrier USS *Ranger*.

During the Battle of Casablanca, gunfire from USS *Massachusetts* struck the French passenger liner *Porthos*, causing her to capsize at her dock in Casablanca. Docked adjacent to her was *Jean Bart*, the bow of which is to the upper right.

The capsized *Porthos* is viewed from astern. Twenty-four persons were killed on the ship.

A hit on the foredeck of *Jean Bart* severely buckled the hull plates. A 16-inch shell from *Massachusetts* struck turret 1, jamming the traversing mechanism and rendering the guns useless.

The starboard side of the hull above the waterline to the front of turret 1 of *Jean Bart* was blown out.

In addition to being struck by 16-inch shells from *Massachusetts*, several bombs from US Navy aircraft hit the ship. One of them tore out the starboard side of the hull adjacent to the rear of the superstructure.

After the Battle of Casablanca, an aerial photographer recorded this view of Casablanca Harbor, with the French warship *Frondeur* (T-22) capsized alongside the *Tempête* (T-52).

A number of French naval ships sortied out of Casablanca Harbor during the battle, including the destroyer *Milan*. After being hit by gunfire from several US ships, *Milan* was beached, as seen in this photograph taken after the battle.

Four days after the Naval Battle of Casablanca, on November 13, 1942, USS *Massachusetts* departed from the area and began her return voyage to the United States. In between periods of modernizations and repairs in Boston in late November, early December, and early January to early February 1943, the ship conducted training and battle-maneuver exercises in Casco Bay, Maine. This photo, taken from USS *Alabama* (BB-60) in December 1942 or January 1943, shows her sister ship Massachusetts at anchor in the background. The blimp above *Alabama*'s yardarm was simulating an aerial attack on the ships.

Massachusetts departed from Casco Bay on February 6, 1943, en route to her new assignment in the Pacific theater of war. She arrived at Cristobal Harbor, Panama, on February 11. The following day, the battleship began the westbound transit of the Panama Canal. This view from the superstructure, facing forward, shows the ship in one of the canal's locks. A very close examination of this photo, published in the ship's World War II cruise book, reveals that a quadruple 40 mm gun mount has been installed on the rear of the top of turret 2; the muzzle ends of the gun barrels are visible at the bottom of the photo. On the center front of the top of turret 2 is a box-shaped splinter shield, which housed a Mk. 51 director for the quadruple 40 mm gun mount.

USS *Massachusetts* is in the background of this original color photograph taken from the afterdeck of USS *Alabama* (BB-60) during a period in Casco Bay, Maine, in January 1943.

During the passage through one of the locks of the Panama Canal, USS *Massachusetts*' mainmast, the aft fire-control tower, turret 3, and three OS2U Kingfisher observation planes spotted on the fantail are viewed from the forward fire-control tower. Toward the lower left is the top of the smokestack.

CHAPTER 3
Massachusetts Moves to the Pacific

On February 18, *Massachusetts* crossed the equator, her log noting, "1805[,] His Majesty King Neptune and Royal Party came on board and was received by the Commanding Officer. Due to present operations[,] all ceremonies were dispensed with. 1806[,] darkened ship."

The ship's log for the next day indicates that *Massachusetts* again had aboard three Kingfisher spotting planes, BuNos 5805, 5432, and 1431, with all three being used for patrols.

On March 4, *Massachusetts* dropped her anchor at Noumea, New Caledonia, in the South Pacific, having steamed 9,000 miles from Casco Bay.

Massachusetts was assigned to Battleship Division 6, part of Task Force 64, commanded by VAdm. Willis Lee. In addition to *Massachusetts*, Battleship Division 6 consisted of USS *Washington* (BB-56), flagship; USS *North Carolina* (BB-55); and USS *Indiana* (BB-58). On March 7, Kingfisher 01431 was reassigned to Naval Air Station, Noumea, and on March 31, Kingfisher 5432 was transferred to Naval Air Station, Noumea.

After a month of brief training cruises and exercises, on April 7, *Massachusetts*, *Washington*, and *Indiana* put to sea escorting the carrier *Saratoga* (CV-3) into the Coral Sea, with *North Carolina* having departed Noumea on March 18. The force did not make contact with the enemy and returned to Noumea on March 29.

On May 26, *Massachusetts* exchanged her Kingfisher 5805 for 1481 from the Naval Air Pool Noumea and, on the twenty-eighth, received aircraft 1480 from the same station.

On June 27, *Massachusetts* got underway as a unit of Task Force 36.3 (Task Force 10 and Task Force 14 combined). Central to the task force were *Saratoga* and HMS *Victorious*, with *Indiana*, *North Carolina*, *San Diego* (CL-53), *San Juan* (CL-54), and thirteen destroyers providing escort. The force went to sea to support Operation Cartwheel, the landing of the 43rd Infantry Division at New Georgia, Solomon Islands, on June 30. The ships were to provide a bulwark against a possible incursion by the Japanese fleet based at Truk. Fortunately, such an incursion did not occur, and on July 25, Task Force 36.3 returned to the Noumea anchorage.

On August 1, Task Force 36.3, sans *Victorious*, steamed for Efate Island, New Hebrides, mooring at Berth 6 at 1432. *Massachusetts* and her crew conducted various exercises in the Efate area until Monday, August 30, when at 1056 she left port with *Saratoga* as part of Task Force 38. *Massachusetts*, along with the rest of the task force, returned to Efate on September 5, without the battleship ever having engaged the enemy.

The remainder of September, as well as all of October up to the last day, was spent either in harbor at Efate or on short training voyages in the immediate area. That changed at 0750 on Sunday, October 31, when she got underway, bound for the Fiji Islands. *Massachusetts*, by then well known to the crew as the Mighty Massy or, alternately, Big Mamie, moored at Berth 49, Nandi Bay, Viti Levu, Fiji Islands, at 1104 on November 7.

On November 11, *Massachusetts* left Fiji in company with Task Group 50.2, which included USS *Washington*, and later joined with Battleship Divisions 6 and 8, creating Task Group 50.2.3, a formidable armada consisting of both the North Carolina–class battleships and all four of the South Dakota–class battleships. This force was made even more impressive on Monday, November 15, when they rendezvoused with Task Force 50, which included nine aircraft carriers. RAdm. Charles Pownall, aboard *Yorktown* (CV-10), assumed tactical command of the force.

On November 19, *Massachusetts*, as well as the rest of Battleship Division 8, along with *Enterprise* (CV-6), *Belleau Wood* (CVL-24), and *Monterey* (CVL-26) and their escorting destroyers, were split off, forming Task Group 50.2. Task Group 50.2 stood 70 miles southeast of Makin Island as the carrier-borne aircraft launched nine strikes against Makin that day in advance of the landing of the 27th Infantry Division. Additional airstrikes were made on

November 20, the day the US Army went ashore. The landing was further supported with a naval bombardment, delivered by veteran battleships USS *Pennsylvania* (BB-38), *New Mexico* (BB-40), and *Mississippi* (BB-41).

Massachusetts and the rest of the task group continued operating in the Gilberts for some time as the Allies struck Tarawa and Apamama. On Thanksgiving evening, Thursday, November 25, the force came under night attack from twenty-seven Japanese aircraft from Roi, many of which dropped illumination flares. During this attack, *Massachusetts'* radar-guided starboard 5-inch mounts fired at the Japanese raiders as they passed the 4,000-yard range mark. Mighty Massy fired eighteen rounds in ninety seconds, the first time her guns had fired on an enemy since leaving the Atlantic. The rounds were fired with flashless powder, while the captain held fire of the 20 mm batteries out of concern that the muzzle flashes would clearly reveal the position of the ship, and the 40 mm batteries remained silent since they were without radar directors.

The next night, thirty-one Japanese aircraft from Roi repeated their attack on the task group, and the gunners aboard *Massachusetts* repeated their actions of the night before, this time firing 147 rounds, again using flashless powder. In addition to the aerial attack, the Japanese had several submarines in the area, one of which had sunk the escort carrier USS *Liscome Bay* (CVE-56) on the morning of November 24. The carrier was lost, along with 644 personnel. The loss of this ship from the task force heightened the awareness of lurking submarines among the men of *Massachusetts* and the other ships in the force.

Massachusetts and her consorts operated in the Gilbert Island area through the end of the month, serving as a deterrent to any counterattack considered by the Japanese.

On the first day of December, *Massachusetts*, as well as *Indiana*, *North Carolina*, and Destroyer Division 92, began to steam the 200 miles to Makin. At 0957 that day, a crewman went overboard, and *Massachusetts* made emergency signals to the screening ships. The escorting USS Boyd reported that the man was recovered 1007. After this "swim," the man was returned to BB-59 at 1302 by breeches buoy.

On December 5 the fleet oiler USS *Neosho* came alongside and transferred 6,908 barrels of bunker fuel to *Massachusetts* by hose, while at the same time, *Massachusetts* transferred to the tanker, which would be returning to port much sooner than the battleship, bags of US mail as well as eight empty oil drums, twenty 5-inch/51-caliber catapult powder tanks with empty cartridge

In a photo taken in the harbor at Noumea, New Caledonia, around April 1943, the battleship in the left distance is either USS *Massachusetts* or her sister ship USS *Indiana* (BB-58). *Massachusetts* frequently was anchored in that harbor from March to May 1943, while performing convoy-escort duties to the Solomon Islands. *Naval History and Heritage Command*

cases, and 291 empty 5-inch/38-caliber powder tanks with empty cartridge cases "for appropriate disposal."

The next day, *Massachusetts* and the rest of Task Unit 50.2.5 rendezvoused with Task Group 50.4 to form Task Group 50.8, consisting of Battleship Division 6 (USS *Washington* and *North Carolina*), Battleship Division 8 (USS *Massachusetts* and *Indiana*), and Battleship Division 9 (USS *South Dakota* and *Alabama*), along with the carriers *Bunker Hill* and *Monterey* and escorts. This formidable force was dispatched to attack the island of Nauru, source of much of Japan's phosphate, as well as home to a Japanese airfield.

At 0609 on December 8, the battleships formed a battle line and, seven minutes later, observed what was determined to be antiaircraft fire from the island being put up against the carrier planes. At 0702, all the battleships simultaneously launched nine-gun salvos against their assigned targets on the island, hurling 74 tons of shells skyward. At 0732, *Massachusetts* ceased fire, having fired 135 16-inch and 400 5-inch rounds at her assigned targets. At 0741, all the ships ceased fire, the bombardment having been concluded. *Massachusetts* was once again unscathed, but Boyd, salvor of the Mamie's errant crewman a week before, took two portside hits from a Japanese shore battery, inflicting severe damage and worse, killing one officer and eleven men of her crew and wounding eight more. Boyd, along with *Alabama* and a smattering of other ships, initially retired to Espiritu Santos for temporary repairs before Boyd returned stateside.

Massachusetts, as well as the other heavies of BatDivs 5, 8, and 9 (less *Alabama*), steamed for Efate, New Hebrides, arriving on December 12.

Upon arrival in Havannah Harbor, Efate Island, New Hebrides, *Massachusetts* was refueled to capacity. On December 16, her ammunition was replenished by the ammunition auxiliary *Rainier* (AE-5), with the ship taking on 110 16-inch high-capacity projectiles, 143 16-inch charges, 643 5-inch/38-caliber Mk. 28 projectiles, 225 5-inch/38-caliber projectiles with Mk. 32 fuse, 52 5-inch/38-caliber illumination rounds, and 863 5-inch/38-caliber charges. Also taken aboard were 11,200 40 mm cartridges and 10,980 20 mm cartridges. The next day, *Massachusetts* took on a further 110 16-inch charges from USS *Alabama*.

On December 22, 1943, *Massachusetts* requested a forty-eight-hour availability in order to replace her SC-1 radar with an SC-2 set, which included the installation of an extension on the foremast. This work was completed at 0500 on Christmas Eve and tested satisfactorily. On Christmas Day, Massachusetts was forced to request a second forty-eight-hour availability due to a failure that had caused excessive oil pressure in the training motor for turret

2, which had caused the housing to bulge, resulting in leakage. Those repairs were completed at 1600 on December 27.

New Year's Day found *Massachusetts* remaining moored in Havannah Harbor, where she remained for several days. On January 7, the William Ward Burrows (AP-6) came alongside and delivered 249 16-inch/45-caliber Mk. 13 Mod. 1 high-capacity projectiles and 502 16-inch/45-caliber reduced charges. Two days later, Burrows returned with a further sixty-three 16-inch/45-caliber Mk. 13 Mod. 1 high-capacity projectiles, and these were augmented on January 13, when a lighter came alongside to deliver seven 16-inch armor-piercing rounds along with their powder charges.

On January 14, *Massachusetts* steamed from her anchorage to conduct a two-day training exercise. During the course of the exercise, there were three firing runs; during the first she expended 104 rounds of 5-inch AA (antiaircraft) common, 2,596 rounds of 40 mm ammunition, and 1,862 rounds of 20 mm ammunition. A second run, beginning at 1156, consumed seven 16-inch rounds and a further 156 5-inch AA common, while the third run, which began at 1428 and involved firing on a drone, discharged ninety-eight 5-inch AA common and seventy-two rounds of 40 mm, ending when the drone crashed at 1440.

Massachusetts returned to Havannah Harbor on January 15, refueled, and remained at anchor until January 18, when she steamed for Funafuti Atoll with Task Group 37.1, which included BatDivs 6, 8, and 9 (less *Alabama*) and escorting destroyers, anchoring at her destination on January 20.

At that time, Task Force 37 was dissolved and Task Group 58.5 was formed, with RAdm. W. A. Lee Jr. commanding. This armada consisted of the following:

Task Unit 58.5.1
BatDiv 6 (*Washington, North Carolina*)
BatDiv 7 (*Iowa, New Jersey*)
BatDiv 8 (*Indiana, Massachusetts*)
BatDiv 9 (*South Dakota, Alabama*)

Task Unit 58.5.5
Bunker Hill
Monterey

Task Unit 58.5.2
Chester
Pensacola
Salt Lake City

Task Unit 58.5.4
DesRon 46
DesDiv 15
DesDiv 95 (*less Steinkel*)

Task Unit 58.5.6
Lackawanna

Over the following two days, *Massachusetts'* fuel bunkers were topped off with 8,607 barrels of oil, and a further 2,807 5-inch rounds and 9,376 40 mm cartridges were added to her magazines.

About an hour past noon on January 22, the main float of one of *Massachusetts'* airplanes was damaged while the plane was taking off. The plane was beached and turned over to the commander at Naval Base Funafuti for salvage or repair. Kingfisher 01511 was transferred from Iowa as a replacement.

At 0754 on January 23, *Massachusetts*, in company with Task Group 58.5, steamed from Funafuti to rendezvous with Task Force 58, which happened early in the morning of January 25. Task Force 58 was then divided into four carrier task groups: 58.1, 58.2, 58.3, and 58.4. *Massachusetts*, along with *Indiana* and supporting unit flagship *Washington*, were assigned to Task Group 58.1, which centered on *Enterprise*, *Yorktown*, and *Belleau Wood*, all of which were supporting the US Marine landings of Operation Flintlock on Kwajalein and Eniwetok. At 1015 on January 30, *Massachusetts* opened fire on Kwajalein from a range of 11,000 yards. Four minutes later, the Japanese began returning fire from a 5-inch battery; their initial rounds fell 150 yards short, but subsequently the Japanese began straddling first the wake of *Massachusetts*, then the ship itself. This brought the ire not only of *Massachusetts*, but also *Washington* and *Indiana*, with the trio of battlewagons bringing the enemy battery under fire of their 5-inch mounts. By 1039 the Japanese battery had been silenced.

By 1115 the initial fifty-seven-salvo phase of the bombardment was complete, with the second phase beginning forty-five minutes later. In the first half hour of the second phase, *Massachusetts* fired twenty-four salvos at Ebeye Island, which were followed by sixty salvos at Kwajelein by 1344. In total, *Massachusetts* fired 362 16-inch high-capacity rounds and 1,902 5-inch/38-caliber rounds at Ebeye and Kwajelein. Although the enemy had failed to hit *Massachusetts*, she was far from unscathed by the operation. Blast damage from the big guns firing had sprung or blown off over twenty doors, damaged light bulkheads, and torn away almost two dozen ventilator ducts.

In the very early morning of the next day, *Massachusetts'* sister *Indiana* collided with supporting unit flagship USS *Washington*,

This photo of *Massachusetts* cruising along a coastline bears the date August 5, 1943. According to the ship's war diary, on that date, *Massachusetts* was at sea with Task Force 38, mooring at Berth 6 in Havannah Harbor, Efate Island, New Hebrides, at 1432 that day. A small, single-stack vessel is on the far side of the battleship's bow.

USS *Massachusetts* is at anchor in the harbor at Efate Island in August 1943. A torpedo net is being set up to the port side of the ship. *Massachusetts* exhibits the Measure 22 camouflage scheme the ship was painted in during October 1942. It consisted of Navy Blue (5-N) on the hull up to the lowest point of the sheer (that is, the lowest point of the main deck), and Haze Gray (5-H) on all vertical surfaces above the top of the sheer. The ship would remain in that camouflage scheme until 1947.

causing extensive damage and forcing both crippled battleships to withdraw to Makin. This left *Massachusetts* as the sole battleship in Task Group 58.1 until the next day, when *North Carolina*, previously assigned to Task Group 58.2, arrived as reinforcement. The reinforcement proved unneeded, since late the next afternoon, February 3, the commander of assault forces released Task Group 58.1 since air support was no longer required. Accordingly, the task group, including *Massachusetts*, began steaming for Majuro Island, Marshall Islands, where they were joined by Task Groups 58.2 and 58.3 as well as tankers. In Majuro Island Lagoon on February 4, *Massachusetts* took on 970,246 gallons of bunker fuel from USS *Neosho*.

On February 5, *Massachusetts* swapped her OS2N-1 BuNo 01481 in exchange for the crippled *Washington*'s OS2U-3 BuNo 05286.

On February 12, *Massachusetts* steamed from Majuro Harbor along with *Iowa*, *New Jersey*, *North Carolina*, *South Dakota*, and *Alabama* as part of Task Unit 58.2.1, supporting three carriers—their objective, the Japanese forces at Truk. After rendezvousing with other units, the task unit arrived at the initial point for the attack at 0642 on February 16, at which time the carriers began launching fighters. At 1702, *Massachusetts* launched her aircraft to rescue the pilot of a downed fighter from USS *Cowpens*, and Lt. C. C. Ainsworth, despite landing his Kingfisher in unfavorable conditions, was able to rescue Lt. (jg) Raffman and return him to *Massachusetts*, being hoisted aboard at 2003.

On February 18, *Massachusetts* and the rest of the Truk strike force steamed to rendezvous with Task Group 50.17.6 to prepare for Operation Gateway, the attack on Saipan in the Marianas. The Allied force was spotted by a Japanese aircraft at 1330 on February 21, 1944, and thus the element of surprise was lost. Five waves of Japanese aircraft began attacking the task force at 2257. The first four waves attacked other task groups, but the fifth wave concentrated on *Massachusetts*' task group. *North Carolina* downed one of the attackers, with *Massachusetts* claiming another, using 74 5-inch rounds. No damage was incurred by *Massachusetts*, whose war diary entry for February 22 included, "The mission of the GATEWAY Operation was completed in three strikes and retirement on course 090-degrees (T) at speed of 25 knots was commenced at 1641."

At 1006 on February 26, *Massachusetts* passed the entrance buoys for Majuro Harbor, and an hour and five minutes later she anchored at Berth A-25. Over the next few days, various types of ammunition were transferred to and from the ship, and on March 9, she took to sea for a few hours for antiaircraft gunnery training.

On March 22, she again got underway as part of Task Force 58, attached to Task Unit 58.9.1, as part of Operation Desecrate, the invasion of Palau. The force reached Palau on March 30, having engaged a couple of Japanese Betty bombers the day prior. At 0635 the US carriers began launching their strike aircraft for the first of six raids against Palau that day. That night, Japanese aircraft attempted a counterattack but were wholly ineffective.

During November 1943, *Massachusetts* escorted Carrier Task Group 50.2 during raids on Japanese forces in the Gilbert Islands, including the islands of Tarawa, Makin, and Abemama. This was in support of the Marine Corps's landings on Tarawa and Makin. In this photo of *Massachusetts* underway during that month, faintly visible to the upper right is a flight of thirteen carrier-based aircraft.

An aerial photo of *Massachusetts* en route to an attack on Taroa Island, Maloelap Atoll, in the Marshall Islands on January 27, 1944, illustrates the compactness of the secondary gun batteries around the superstructure. This was owing to the relatively short (fore and aft) length of the superstructure, compared to other US battleships. In addition to five twin 5-inch/38-caliber gun mounts on each side of the superstructure, there were also quadruple 40 mm and single 20 mm gun mounts around the superstructure and the decks. Present on the top of turret 3 is a quadruple 40 mm gun mount in a drum-shaped splinter shield, flanked by a single 20 mm gun mount and splinter shield on each side. Toward the front of the turret top is the associated Mk. 51 director, with a stack of life rafts to its rear.

More airstrikes were made on Palau on the next day, as well as a raid on Yap.

On April 1, 1944, *Massachusetts* and the rest of Task Group 58.3 advanced on Woleai Island. While US forces reported sixteen Japanese Betty aircraft airborne over Woleai, all were downed by the American aircraft striking the island, with none of the enemy aircraft reaching the task group. In fact, as the task group began to retire to Majuro Atoll, *Massachusetts'* deck log noted, "Set Condition of Readiness II-Able as imminence of an air attack improbable."

The task group entered the Majuro Atoll anchorage at 0900 on April 6. On April 8, while at the anchorage, there was a change of command of *Massachusetts*, with Capt. T. D. Ruddock being relieved by Capt. W. W. Warlick. Capt. Ruddock had been promoted to rear admiral and given command of Battleship Division 4, with USS *Colorado* (BB-45) as flagship.

On April 13, Task Force 58, with *Massachusetts* still assigned to Task Group 58.3, once again got underway, this time to support Task Force 77 in its upcoming operations against New Guinea and the amphibious assault on Hollandia. D-day was set for April 22, 1944, and the day before the aircraft of Task Group 58.3 began their strikes at 0655, continuing until 1806.

The landings began at dawn of the twenty-second, with air support beginning at 0618, and continued throughout the day. After multiple airstrikes and multiple interceptions of enemy aircraft, many at night, on April 24 the commander of Task Force 77 reported that air operations by Task Force 58 were no longer required. Task Force 58 lingered in the area of Humboldt Bay for a few days, the carrier aircraft downing multiple intruding Japanese aircraft, with the escorting destroyers picking up and making prisoners of war many Japanese aviators.

On April 27, USS *Caperton* (DD-650) came alongside, delivering officer messenger mail instructing that Task Force 58 was retiring from the Humboldt Bay area and setting course for yet another carrier airstrike on Truk. En route, *Massachusetts*, with escorting destroyers *Converse* (DD-509) and *Thatcher* (DD-514), were diverted to Seadler Harbor to rendezvous with *Indiana* (BB-58). RAdm. Davis transferred his flag from *Massachusetts* to *Indiana*, which was freshly repaired from her collision with *Washington* (BB-56) on February 1. At 1732 on April 28, the two battleships, along with their four escorting destroyers, steamed from Seadler Harbor, rejoining the rest of Task Group 58.3 on the morning of April 29 (while still in east longitude), steaming for Truk.

The next day, at 0000, all clocks of Task Force 58 were set back twenty-four hours as the force passed into west longitude (zone +12) time, and at 0717 the carrier aircraft launched their initial strike against Truk. The enemy had spotted the US fleet and launched intercepting aircraft, a flight of Oscars, one of which approached Task Group 58.3 and was repelled by antiaircraft fire from *Enterprise* (CV-6) early in the morning. At 1552 a TBF crashed 2,500 yards off *Massachusetts'* port bow, with *Ingersoll* (DD-652) picking up survivors. Pritchett (DD-561) also picked up a downed aviator, Lt. F. A. Levine, from *Lexington* (CV-16), who was suspected of having a skull fracture and was transferred to *Massachusetts*, since she had far-more-advanced medical facilities and staff than did the destroyer.

Additional airstrikes were launched against Truk the next day, and on May 1, Task Force 58 began retiring to Majuro Island. However, en route to their anchorage the force would pass Japanese-held Ponape Island, a 129-square-mile island that was bypassed in the Allied island-hopping strategy. The task force had been directed to unleash a surface bombardment by the battleships as well as aerial bombardment on the garrison of about eight thousand Japanese troops and sailors on Ponape and its smaller outlying islands as the armada passed by. This bombardment began at 1530, when the first of six planned twenty-minute firing periods began. *Massachusetts*, along with *Indiana* and *North Carolina*, was assigned to Bombardment Group 2. During each firing period, two battleships would conduct bombardment while the third stood ready for counterbattery fire. *Massachusetts* was assigned counterbattery duty during firing periods 2 and 5. During firing period 1, she was assigned the Japanese seaplane base on Langer Island as her target, with her first salvo fired at 1530 and landing in the target area. Just over two hours later, following firing period 4, the commander of the striking force ordered a ceasefire, since no suitable targets remained. *Massachusetts* had fired eighty-seven 16-inch rounds as well as twenty-nine rounds from her 5-inch secondary battery.

While en route to Majuro Atoll on May 2, Lt. F. A. Levine, the downed *Lexington* aviator who had been brought aboard with a suspected skull fracture, and Lt. (jg) C. L. Lofton, who had been rescued from inside Truk lagoon by *Massachusetts'* Lt. Ainsworth, left the ship via breeches buoy to Thatcher (DD-514), which ferried the aviators back to their ships.

At 0906 on May 4, *Massachusetts* anchored at Berth 76 in Majuro Atoll and the next day transferred 495 rounds of 5-inch/38-caliber projectiles each to *New Jersey* and *Iowa*. She also transferred Kingfisher 01413 to *Iowa* and received 5606 in exchange.

On May 6, *Massachusetts*, as part of Task Group 58.7, steamed for Pearl Harbor in company with *Yorktown* and Destroyer Squadron 6, joining *Princeton* and *Monterey* on this voyage.

During a battle a battleship could expend an enormous amount of ammunition. After one such engagement, hundreds of spent cartridge cases are scattered on the main deck around several of the 5-inch/38-caliber gun mounts. Since a single 5-inch/38-caliber gun could fire one round every three seconds when operating fully automatically, a twin mount could consume up to forty powder casings every minute.

Of keen interest in this undated photo of an admiral's inspection on the starboard side of the quarterdeck of USS *Massachusetts* is the unusual gun mount in the tub to the far right. This was an Elco Thunderbolt quadruple antiaircraft gun mount. Developed for use on PT boats, Thunderbolts also were mounted experimentally on some battleships. Various combinations of .50-caliber machine guns and 20 mm guns were employed in the Thunderbolt; this one had four 20 mm guns. To the upper right is the left rear corner of turret 3.

An Elco Thunderbolt armed with four 20 mm guns is on a pallet on a wharf. For elevating the guns, the armored tub pivoted on two trunnions, which were attached to a base that rotated, for training the guns in azimuth. *PT Boats, Inc.*

The same Thunderbolt is viewed from the right rear, showing the seat back for the gunner to the let. Three of the magazines for the staggered 20 mm guns are visible inside. On the curved rear of the tub are round cutouts for the rears of two of the guns, below which are two ejector chutes for spent casings. *PT Boats, Inc.*

Upon entering Pearl Harbor on May 11, *Massachusetts* tied up alongside *Colorado* and *Washington* and, per her log, "commenced loading spare parts and navy yard overhaul material in storage for this vessel at Pearl Harbor Navy Yard."

The next day, *Massachusetts*, escorted by *Thorn* (DD-647) and *LeHardy* (DE-20), began the welcome voyage to Puget Sound Navy Yard, Bremerton, Washington. At 1705 on May 19, *Massachusetts* dropped anchor in Sinclair Inlet, Bremerton, and began offloading ammunition prior to entering drydock. The unloading was completed at 0515 the next morning, and she entered drydock 5 at 1358 for a well-earned overhaul. She remained on keel blocks in the drydock until June 25, when she was floated and towed to Berth 3-D, where yard work was continued through July 3. Included in the yard work were considerable enhancements to *Massachusetts*' antiaircraft batteries, as well as her radar and fire control suite. The 20 mm battery was reduced from fifty-two to thirty-two single mounts, a move in part to compensate for the increase of 40 mm armament from sixteen to eighteen quad mounts. In addition, she was fitted with a twin 20 mm mount as well as an Elco Thunderbolt quad 20 mm mount.

Massachusetts' main battery got improved fire control as a result of replacing the Mk. 3 fire control radar atop the Mk. 38

Several times in her service career, USS *Massachusetts* was forced to navigate through severe storms, including a major typhoon in December 1944. This view from the superstructure was taken during a severe storm, with waves crashing on her starboard bow. The two quadruple 40 mm gun mounts installed on the foredeck in mid-1944, with their prominent splinter shields, are not present, indicating the photo precedes the installation of those mounts.

directors with the superior Mk. 8 units. Also, during the shipyard work, the SC air-search radar set was replaced with an improved model, the SK. Adjacent to the Mk. 4 radars atop the Mk. 37 5-inch gun directors, Mk. 22 "orange peel" elevation-only radar antennas were installed. Additional Mk. 51 directors for the 40 mm mounts were installed amidships. For improved surface search, a second SG set was installed on the top mast, and the ship's original SG antenna was relocated to the new and enlarged mainmast from its former location at the front of the fire control tower.

Below the waterline there was a change in propeller arrangement. *Massachusetts* had been built with four four-blade propellers, but during this yard period the outer propellers were replaced with five-blade units in hopes of lessening vibration, an arrangement initially installed on sister ship *Alabama* the year before.

At 1300 on Independence Day 1944, dock trials of the main engines and auxiliary machinery began and were concluded satisfactorily at 1655.

The next day, she began taking on stores and provisions in preparation for sea trials. Restocking the ship took until July 9, with full-power trials undertaken on July 10. At the end of those trials, she anchored in Sinclair Inlet and began taking on ammunition from Naval Ammunition Depot Puget Sound. This was completed at 0840 on July 14. A couple of hours later, seventy-six shipyard workmen came aboard to do further work on the ship as she steamed to Port Angeles Harbor, Washington, where she arrived at 1636 the next day. Less than three hours after discharging the yard workers, *Massachusetts* made way for Pearl Harbor, where she tied up on July 21, and workmen set out to complete yard work that remained unfinished from her time at Puget Sound.

CHAPTER 4
Taking the War to Japan

On May 20, 1944, *Massachusetts* arrived at Puget Sound Navy Yard, Bremerton, Washington, for a period of modernization and repairs that lasted until early July. This sequence of photos of the ship was taken in Puget Sound on July 11, 1944, after that work was completed. Visible here on the foredeck are two quadruple 40 mm gun mounts and splinter shields, installed at Bremerton. On the forecastle are two single 20 mm guns with splinter shields. A new and taller foremast and mainmast had been installed, with new radar antennas. *US Navy via A. D. Baker III*

On August 1, *Massachusetts*, escorted by four destroyers, got underway for Eniwetok Atoll, which came into sight at 0956 on August 8, anchoring there at 1337.

She would remain at that anchorage until August 30, when she got underway as a component of Task Group 34.10, which included four other fast battleships, Cruiser Divisions 13 and 14, and Destroyer Squadrons 50 and 52. This task group was dissolved on September 3, and the battleships thereafter were organized as Task Group 38.5. A bit of levity came during these operations when, on September 4, the task group crossed the equator and the time-honored tradition of the Neptune party occurred, with the pollywogs becoming shellbacks after, of course, completion of the various rites.

Through September 9, the armada practiced battle line maneuvers and tactical exercises.

On September 11, 1944, Task Group 38.5 was dissolved and *Massachusetts* became part of Task Group 38.3.2, with the heavy-support group for the airstrikes beginning the next day on Leyte, Negros, Cebu, and Samar in the central Philippines. In a lengthy address to the crew on September 12, Capt. Warlick told the men of USS *Massachusetts* not only the nature of their ship's operation, but an overview of the strategy behind the strikes on the islands, concluding by stating:

It is Admiral Halsey's hope that he can smoke out the Japanese fleet in one of these operations. During the early strikes of the carrier task forces, the fast battleships were kept separated for the purpose of training in preparation for the surface action which Admiral Halsey is trying to create. We have accompanied the carriers this time because the enemy has already been alerted and may try to interfere on the present strike. It is doubtful that surface forces will be encountered on this strike, but it is within the capacity of the enemy to resist by air if he is willing to risk his planes. Therefore, we must be particularly alert to repel air attacks for the next three days.

For ten days, *Massachusetts* and the rest of the heavy-support group kept watch over the carriers as their aircraft pummeled the central Philippines. On September 13, *Massachusetts'* 40 mm and 5-inch batteries were among those firing on an Oscar that was downed following its unsuccessful attempt to bomb Princeton. The next day, Lt. G. A. Robinson, in one of *Massachusetts'* Kingfishers, rescued a downed USS *Wasp* airman, returning him to the battleship for subsequent transfer back to Wasp.

On September 20, Capt. Warlick again addressed his crew, saying:

The strikes against the central and southern Philippines were a part of the campaigns to seize Morotai and Palau. There remains still effective in the Philippines the strongest and most important island of the whole group. That island is Luzon, the northernmost. It is at once the most populous, the most powerful[,] and strategically, the most important of all the group. It contains the important harbor of Manila Bay. Around Manila are a great number of airfields, some of them containing as many as eight flying strips. This concentration of power is the objective of our present strike. Tomorrow morning at dawn, the full striking power of Task Force 38 will be concentrated on the Manila Bay district. The purpose is, of course, to destroy first, the air power, then the shipping in the port, then the port installations. . . . It is entirely possible that they may become aware of our approach. If they do, we can expect some interruptions tonight. If not, we can still expect to have to fight off attacks tomorrow. . . . If we are counter-attacked, this task force and the *Massachusetts* will know how to deal with them. I wish I could tell you we might encounter surface forces, but I believe we will not. The time does not appear suitable for them to risk their fleet.

It is probable that the strike will continue for two days. If this strike is as effective as the previous ones, the Philippines will be eliminated as an effective Japanese stronghold. In two days, we will know the answer.

At dawn the next day, the carriers began launching their strikes against Luzon, and on the twenty-fourth, strikes resumed against the central Philippines, and on the day after, the task group began withdrawing to Saipan, where *Massachusetts* dropped anchor on September 28. The respite was brief, since on September 29 she and Task Force 34 weighed anchor and commenced steaming to Ulithi, dropping anchor there at 0708 on October 1, 1944.

The next morning, RAdm. G. B. Davis hoisted his flag aboard *Massachusetts*, thereby making her the flagship of Battleship Division 8, which consisted of *Massachusetts* and *Washington*. *Washington*, incidentally, was flagship of VAdm. W. A. Lee, commander of Task Force 34 and commander of battleships in the Pacific.

During the course of the day, the weather began to deteriorate, and information was received that a tropical disturbance of some intensity was to the north. While *Massachusetts* was taking on fuel from *Cimarron* (AO-22), the battleship was also secured for heavy weather, with preparations made to get underway on one hour's notice. At 1941 the refueling operations were completed, with 350,757 gallons of fuel oil having been pumped aboard.

Due to the storm, on the morning of October 3, Task Force 34 was ordered to sea. The weather conditions made navigation from the anchorage a challenge, with *Massachusetts'* log noting, "During the run down the channel inside the Atoll[,] two Mk. 8 Radars [the main battery fire control radar] were kept on designated targets and ranges taken with them checked with the position of the ship as determined by visual bearings. As the ship neared the entrance channel the weather closed in, making impossible the taking of any new bearings visually. Radar ranges were plotted continuously, and these, together with dead reckoning, furnished what proved to be an accurate plot of the ship's track through the narrow channel."

The Task Force stayed at sea through the day as the storm relented, with winds dropping from force 7 at 0100 to force 5 at 2400 hours. As a result, the task force returned to Ulithi the morning of October 4.

Two days later, on October 6, Task Force 34 was dissolved, and the units of that force, including *Massachusetts*, rejoined Task Force 38, with BB-59 being in Task Group 38.3. Task Group 38.3 got underway at 1643 to support landings in Leyte Gulf, with the first strike being the airfields on Okinawa and Formosa. With complete surprise, the carriers launched attacks on Okinawa on October 10, meeting no resistance. The task force then changed course, steaming toward Formosa. This time, the Japanese were aware of the task force's approach, and the task force came under aerial attack. Twice, *Massachusetts'* antiaircraft batteries opened fire when enemy aircraft came within range, both times driving off the attackers.

October 13 saw more airstrikes on Formosa, with the Japanese again counterattacking, and *Massachusetts'* antiaircraft batteries only briefly going into action at 1842. *Massachusetts* was unscathed, but three minutes later a Japanese torpedo plane scored a hit on USS *Canberra* (CA-70) below the armor belt, flooding her engine room. *Wichita* (CA-45) was detailed to take *Canberra* under tow. The next morning, as *Massachusetts* refueled some of her escorts, she received word that *Houston* (CL-81), which had been protecting *Canberra*, had also been torpedoed, with her damage also in her machinery spaces, disabling the cruiser.

At dusk, two Jills were able to reach *Massachusetts'* formation but were brought down by her gunners. A third aircraft of the type crashed into the antiaircraft cruiser *Reno* (CL-96), hitting on her fantail, causing damage and inflicting causalities.

These events would alter the plan, if not the mission, of *Massachusetts* and the rest of the task force. Capt. Warlick addressed the battleship's crew at 1720 on October 16, saying,

Admiral Halsey has made a change in plans for our Task Force. This change has been brought about by the enemy's reaction to our sustained strikes on Formosa, or rather it has been brought about by the enemy's opinion of the effectiveness of his counter-attacks upon us.

The shapes of the new foremast and mainmast are evident in this view of the starboard side of the ship. The mainmast remained a single-pole type, although considerably taller than the original mast, while the foremast, originally a single pole, now comprised a lower mast and a topmast that was offset to the rear. The new air-search radar antenna was positioned on a platform midway up the foremast. *US Navy via A. D. Baker III*

You all are aware of the statements of damage to us which have been broadcast from Tokyo. Admiral Halsey has reason to believe that the enemy really thinks he has defeated us and may come out to try and [*sic*] mop up the remainder. Let's hope they do. We are prepared . . .

The enemy apparently believes that he has sunk fifty-three of our ships, including seventeen carriers. As we all know, that is all the carriers we brought along . . .

To our own gunners I express the admiration of the whole ship's company for their demonstration of how the watch should handle a torpedo plane attack . . .

Last night, after fueling, instead of moving toward the Philippines, we moved north. We are now 250 miles south of Okinawa and 400 miles east of Formosa. The damaged cruisers and their escorts are southwest of us; therefore, it is apparent that Admiral Halsey has moved Task Force 38 to a position where it can make a flank attack upon any enemy surface force leaving Japan to attack that group.

The Japanese, intent on holding the Philippines, had initiated an elaborate plan designed to annihilate the US invasion force. Like Capt. Warlick, the Japanese were itching for a surface action, and their plans were engineered to bring this into being.

The Japanese armada dispatched to secure the Philippines consisted of the Northern Force, Central Force, and Southern Force, to use the terminology assigned by the US Navy. The Northern Force, with the fleet carrier *Zuikaku*, three light carriers, two hybrid battleship/aircraft carriers, three cruisers, and eight destroyers, was a sacrificial decoy force. Only 116 aircraft were distributed among the various carriers of this force, which was intended to lure Halsey away from Leyte Gulf—a strategy that, in short, worked.

This distraction was intended to allow the powerful First Mobile Striking Force, referred to by the Allies as the Central Force, with its five battleships, including the largest two ever built—*Yamato* and *Musashi*, twelve cruisers, and fifteen destroyers, to enter San Bernardino Strait and attack Adm. Kinkaid's Seventh Fleet, which was there to support the Allied landing on Leyte.

Ironically, US reconnaissance failed to spot the decoy Northern Force, but US submarines *Darter* and *Dace* did observe and attack the Central Force just after midnight on October 23, and the next day the Southern Force, which consisted of two battleships, four cruisers, and eleven destroyers bound for Surigao Strait, was observed as well.

Task Group 38.3 lingered east of Manila, a position that allowed it both to conduct air operations against the Northern

Visayas, which began on October 21, as well as to intercept Japanese surface forces.

The next two days were uneventful, but on October 24, Japanese aircraft located Task Group 38.3, and a Yokosuka D4Y Judy based on Luzon dove out of the clouds, targeting one of the ships under the watch of *Massachusetts*, the Independence-class carrier *Princeton* (CVL-23), striking the light carrier with a single bomb between the elevators. Unfortunately, the carrier was in the process of refueling her aircraft, which had just returned. Six aircraft in the hangar, laden with ordnance and drop tanks, ignited, and the fire soon engulfed the hangar deck, the blast having ruptured the fire mains.

Princeton was mortally wounded by the attack, and a munitions explosion aboard the carrier heavily damaged *Birmingham* (CL-62) and two destroyers that had come alongside to assist with firefighting and rescue efforts. Thereafter, the stricken carrier was scuttled, *Princeton* thus becoming the first ship lost while under the protection of *Massachusetts'* antiaircraft batteries.

Massachusetts' log recorded that "USS BIRMINGHAM, MORRISON, IRWIN and GATLING had left the formation en route to Ulithi because of the damage done by explosions aboard the USS PRINCETON."

About an hour after *Princeton* was hit, the Japanese Central Force came under attack from aircraft from *Intrepid* and *Cabot*, followed by a second wave from the same ships joined by additional aircraft from *Essex* and *Lexington*. A third wave arrived later from *Enterprise* and *Franklin*. However, the bulk of these efforts were directed solely at the battleship *Musashi*, which was sunk, and the cruiser *Myoko*, which was crippled, thus still leaving Japanese admiral Kurita with a powerful force. Kurita reversed course, which Halsey interpreted as a withdrawal, when in fact it was only a maneuver to get beyond the range of the US aircraft and a feint to mislead Halsey. At 1715, Kurita again changed course and steamed through San Bernardino Strait, bearing down on Kinkaid's Seventh Fleet.

Massachusetts and the rest of Halsey's modern fast battleships continued to steam northward, in pursuit of the Japanese decoy force.

The bulk of Japanese Southern Force (Force C), under Vice Admiral Shōji Nishimura, with two old battleships, a heavy cruiser, and four destroyers, steamed through Surigao Strait, intent on joining with Kurita's Central Force in the Leyte Gulf and annihilating Kinkaid's invasion fleet. It was followed, at some distance, by the Japanese Second Striking Force, under the command of Vice Admiral Kiyohide Shima.

US rear admiral Jesse Oldendorf, with Task Group 77.2, a force of six old, slow battleships (five of them survivors of Pearl Harbor), four heavy cruisers, four light cruisers, twenty-eight destroyers, and thirty-nine PT boats, was waiting for the Japanese when

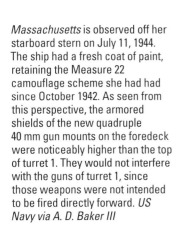

Massachusetts is observed off her starboard stern on July 11, 1944. The ship had a fresh coat of paint, retaining the Measure 22 camouflage scheme she had had since October 1942. As seen from this perspective, the armored shields of the new quadruple 40 mm gun mounts on the foredeck were noticeably higher than the top of turret 1. They would not interfere with the guns of turret 1, since those weapons were not intended to be fired directly forward. *US Navy via A. D. Baker III*

Massachusetts is viewed from astern on July 11, 1944. The recent modernizations included new fire-control radar antennas. The four Mk. 37 secondary-battery directors' existing Mk. 4 antennas were augmented by Mk. 22 height-finder antennas; the Mk. 22s were nicknamed "orange-peel" antennas because their shape was similar to that of the peel of an orange segment. The two Mk. 38 main batteries' original Mk. 3 radar antennas were replaced by the much-superior Mk. 8 antennas.

Nishimura entered the strait. At 2236, the US PT boats began their attacks as the Japanese steadily advanced. A few minutes later, the Japanese column entered a gauntlet of destroyers, who unleashed their torpedoes, striking both of the Japanese battleships, causing Fuso to fall out of the column and sink thereafter.

At 0316, *West Virginia* picked up the advancing Japanese ships on her radar at a range of 42,000 yards. At 0353, when the range had closed to 22,800 yards, she unleashed a broadside at *Yamashiro*, hitting the Japanese battleship. Soon, other ships joined in the melee. By 0420 the second Japanese battleship had sunk, and two Japanese cruisers were retreating. Shima, first encountering US PT boats, then meeting the retreating remnants of Force C, joined them in retreat.

About seven hours before Oldendorf's PT boats launched their attacks on Nishimura's force, Halsey sent a poorly worded signal to his task group commanders and copied Adm. Nimitz at Pearl and Adm. King in Washington, saying,

BATDIV 7 BILOXI, VINCENNES, MIAMI, DESRON 52 LESS STEVEN POTTER, FROM TG 38.2 AND WASHINGTON, ALABAMA, WICHITA, NEW ORLEANS, DESDIV 100, PATTERSON, BAGLEY FROM TG 38.4 WILL BE FORMED AS TASK FORCE 34 UNDER VICE ADMIRAL LEE, COMMANDER BATTLE LINE. TF 34 TO ENGAGE DECISIVELY AT LONG RANGES. CTG 38.4 CONDUCT CARRIERS OF TG 38.2 AND TG 38.4 CLEAR OF SURFACE FIGHTING. INSTRUCTIONS FOR TG 38.3 AND TG 38.1 LATER. HALSEY, OTC IN NEW JERSEY

Strangely, Halsey did not copy Adm. Kinkaid, who was directly impacted by this. Nonetheless, Kinkaid's radio staff had picked up the message and passed it along to Kinkaid. However, because of the ambiguous language that Halsey used, everyone receiving the message—from Nimitz to Kinkaid—interpreted it to be saying that Task Force 34 HAD been formed and dispatched. About two hours later, Halsey sent a clarifying message by voice transmission, saying, "IF THE ENEMY SORTIES [through San Bernardino Strait] TF 34 WILL BE FORMED WHEN DIRECTED BY ME."

However, voice transmissions at the time lacked the range of the original telegraphic message; thus neither Kinkaid nor, notably, Admiral Nimitz got this clarification. Thus, the powerful Task Force 38 continued to steam north through the night, including all the battleships and cruisers to be detached as Task Force 34, when directed by Halsey. This left San Bernardino Strait unguarded against Vice Admiral Takeo Kurita's still-powerful Central Force.

At 0300 on October 25, Kurita passed through San Bernardino Strait and proceeded along the coast of Samar to intercept Kinkaid's transports and landing craft, with only Seventh Fleet's three escort carrier units (call signs "Taffy" 1, 2, and 3) and their escorting destroyers and destroyer escorts separating the powerful four-battleship, eight-cruiser, and eleven-destroyer Japanese surface fleet from the essentially unarmed and armored invasion force. Each of the Casablanca-class escort carriers mounted a single 5-inch dual-purpose gun, eight twin 40 mm guns, and twenty 20 mm guns. Each could accommodate, at maximum, thirty aircraft.

Shortly after dawn, Kurita encountered "Taffy 3"—RAdm. Clifton Sprague's Task Unit 77.4.3, with its six escort carriers, three destroyers, and four destroyer escorts. At 0650, Sprague ordered his aircraft launched and the carriers to rush for cover in a nearby rain squall. The hopelessly outgunned and outnumbered destroyers of Taffy 3 rushed forward to engage the Japanese. Despite one of the most valiant defenses ever put forward by a US surface force, there was great concern that the much-heavier armed Japanese force would soon overrun the American ships and thereby have unfettered access to the troop-laden transports of the landing force, as well as risking exposing those Allied troops already ashore to bombardment from the Japanese battleships.

Following the action in Surigao Strait, Kinkaid had signaled Halsey at 0412 seeking assurance that Task Force 34 was in fact protecting San Bernardino Strait. This message was not delivered to Halsey for about two and a half hours. Halsey replied that rather than protecting the strait, TF 34 was with his carriers.

By 0800, Kinkaid was desperate and began sending plain-language messages to Halsey, the first saying, "My situation is critical. Fast battleships and support by airstrikes may be able to keep enemy from destroying CVEs and entering Leyte."

This message was followed by three more from the increasingly frustrated and alarmed Kinkaid:

At 08:22: "Fast Battleships are Urgently Needed Immediately at Leyte Gulf."
At 09:05: "Need Fast Battleships and Air Support."
At 09:07: "4 Battleships, 8 Cruisers Attack Our Escort Carriers."

At 0848, Halsey, still not grasping why he should stop his pursuit to steam toward Kinkaid, rather than leaving their defense to themselves, ordered VAdm. John S. McCain's Task Group 38.1 to make best possible speed to relieve Taffy 3.

At 1000, Kinkaid radioed again, in plain language, "WHERE IS LEE X SEND LEE."

Massachusetts is observed from port and astern; her fire-control tower is obscured by smoke from the stack. Aft of the smokestack are angled braces for the mainmast. The new Mk. 8 fire-control radar antenna atop the aft Mk. 38 director is visible against the sky. *US Navy via A. D. Baker III*

A tugboat is positioned against *Massachusetts'* hull in this photo taken off her port bow. Faintly visible above the platform partway up the foremast is the new SK air-search radar antenna, which measured 17 by 17 feet. Faintly above it near the top of the mainmast is an SG surface-search radar antenna; another SG antenna is on the mainmast, just above the national ensign.

At Pearl Harbor, Adm. Nimitz had seen Kinkaid's pleas and radioed Halsey with the message "WHERE IS RPT WHERE IS TASK FORCE THIRTY FOUR RR THE WORLD WONDERS."

While "the world wonders" was added to the message as part of a routine padding to confuse enemy code breakers, and the initial "where is" was erroneously repeated by a signal operator, this message from Nimitz shook Halsey, who, despite cursing and throwing his hat on the floor, formed Special Task Group 34.5, consisting of BatDiv 7 (*Iowa*, plus his flagship *New Jersey*—the two fastest of the fast battleships present), CruDiv 14, and DesRon 52, and at 1620 began steaming south. Much of Halsey's frustration stemmed from the fact that his fast battleships had almost gotten within gun range of the Japanese Northern Force, and his belief that by the time his battleships could reach San Bernardino, the Japanese would have fled. The rest of TG 38.2, including *Massachusetts*, maintained their northern course until 2316, when they too were ordered to steam south toward Kinkaid.

The various units of the Third Fleet arrived at San Bernardino Strait too late to have any material effect on the battle, with *Massachusetts'* deck log for October 26 noting, "Steaming with Task Group 38.2 en route to rendezvous with Task Group 38.1 and strike position off San Bernardino Strait (Lat. 14°N; Long. 125°E.). At 0500 joined and commenced maneuvering for strike position."

While the guns of *Massachusetts* remained silent against the Central Force, the planes of Task Groups 38.3 and 38.4, under Marc Mitscher, along with the cruisers of RAdm. DuBose, detached from Task Force 34, did essentially destroy the Japanese Northern Force on October 25, the pursuit of which Halsey had abandoned in order to steam to San Bernardino, by air.

The following day, *Massachusetts* and the rest of Task Group 38.2 refueled at sea and, over the period of the next three days, steamed for Ulithi, *Massachusetts* dropping anchor in Berth 7, Ulithi, at 0806 on October 30.

November 1 brought a series of orders to the bridge of *Massachusetts*. First orders were received that Task Group 38.3, which included *Massachusetts*, was to sortie at 1600 and proceed to Manus Island for availability. But at 1400, two hours before scheduled departure, orders were received that BatDiv 8, which was *Massachusetts* and *Alabama*, were to remain in Ulithi, with *Massachusetts* reporting to Task Group 38.1 for temporary duty. Then, at 2310, a message was received from ComTask Force 38 that BatDiv 8 as well as *Ticonderoga* was to prepare to sortie as

The demarcation between the dark shade of the Navy Blue on the hull below the anchors and the lighter shade of Haze Gray on the higher-up surfaces is apparent in this view off the bow of *Massachusetts* on July 11, 1944.

soon as possible, with four destroyers from Task Group 38.3 to serve as escorts. The trio of big ships got underway at 0218 on November 2, cleared the entrance buoys at 0316, and rendezvoused with Task Group 38.3 at 2350.

On November 4, BatDiv 8, *Massachusetts* and *Alabama*, was reassigned to Task Group 38.1, and on November 5 all hands aboard *Massachusetts* stood to air attack stations as aircraft of the task force began striking positions on the island of Luzon, with Task Force 38.1 being assigned the area of Clark Field. *Lexington*, assigned to Task Group 38.2, was struck in the signal bridge by a kamikaze. US intelligence reported that Japanese submarines were operating in the area, and *Massachusetts'* own men detected enemy radio transmissions, with the radio detection finder indicating that they originated from submarines. The men of the fleet were doubly vigilant due to the threats both above and below them.

At dawn on the sixth, the US fleet resumed launching airstrikes, and while enemy aircraft did try to retaliate, unsuccessfully, against Task Group 38.3, *Massachusetts* and Task Group 38.1 faced no enemy aircraft. In late afternoon the task group retired toward a refueling area. At 1100 on November 7, USS *Brush* (DD-745) came alongside *Massachusetts* to starboard, and fourteen minutes later USS *Charrette* (DD-581) came alongside port to refuel. Refueling the destroyers was completed at 1234, and just as they were casting off, a man was reported overboard to port. The two departing destroyers were immediately notified by voice radio, and *Brush* was able to recover the uninjured sailor. At 1325, *Massachusetts* herself came along the port side of the fleet oiler USS *Lackawanna* (AO-40) to be refueled herself. *Massachusetts'* war diary noted, "Heavy seas caused several interruptions, but the operation was completed at 1705."

Those heavy seas were related to other details noted in the war diary: "Reports received concerning a typhoon, the center of which is believed to be approximately 300 miles to the south, are borne out by increasingly heavy seas."

For the next two days, *Massachusetts* and her task group maneuvered to avoid the worst of the weather, with her war diary for November 10 recording, "The typhoon has passed to the south and west of us, and the barometer is rising, although the sea remains heavy."

From November 11 through 14, *Massachusetts* and Task Group 38.1 continued with their mission of pounding the Philippines and Luzon with airstrikes, but for a respite on November 12 for refueling at sea.

After five days of steaming, by November 19 *Massachusetts* and the rest of Task Force 38 were in strike position for a day of further raids on the Luzon-Mindoro area of the Philippines. That evening, the ships began retiring toward Ulithi, reaching the anchorage on November 24. *Massachusetts* and the rest of Task Group 38.1 remained at Ulithi until December 1, when they along with Task Group 38.2 steamed for Mindoro. This operation was short lived. At 1043, *Massachusetts'* no. 1 shaft had to be secured as the result of a bearing overheating. After the machinery was examined, at 1700 a dispatch was sent to the commander of Task Group 38.1 recommending that *Massachusetts* return to Ulithi for repair, if the tactical situation would permit. This recommendation was agreed to, and *Massachusetts* and assigned escorts *Franks* (DD-554) and *Buchanan* (DD-484) set a course back to Ulithi at 1752. Later that day, ComThird Fleet ordered the two task groups to also return to Ulithi. As *Massachusetts* made her way toward Ulithi, her men continued their efforts to repair the overheating bearing, ultimately requesting permission to conduct speed tests, during which its speed was gradually built up to 25 knots prior to entering the atoll. At 1504 she dropped anchor at Berth 38, Urushi Anchorage, Ulithi, remaining there until December 10.

At 0517 on December 10, Task Group 38.1, which still included USS *Massachusetts* and *Alabama* as well as *Yorktown*, *Wasp*, *Cowpens*, and *Monterey*, once again sortied to support landings on Mindoro. En route on December 12, Task Group 38.1 rendezvoused with Task Groups 38.2 and 38.3.

The war diary of *Massachusetts* for December 14 records in part:

> Approaching strike position . . . from where the first of a series of air strikes is to be launched against Japanese aircraft, airfields[,] and facilities on the Island of Luzon at dawn in support of landings on the Island of Mindoro by airborne and amphibious troops under the command of General MacArthur. Our purpose is to neutralize enemy air power in the Northern and Central Philippines and to deny the use of Luzon harbors to enemy combatant and support shipping by means of heavy air strikes against and continuous patrol over all Japanese airfields in the area.
>
> Thirty minutes before sunrise, heavy fighter sweeps were launched in order to catch the enemy by surprise if possible, and to keep his aircraft pinned to the ground. Our fighters evidently were successful in accomplishing this purpose, as very few enemy airborne planes were reported. Fighter sweeps continued throughout the day, no dive bombers or torpedo bombers were launched as the primary target of the days sweeps is enemy aircraft.

Massachusetts executes a hard turn to port off Point Wilson, on the Olympic Peninsula in Washington, on July 11, 1944. Turret 1 is trained to starboard, and the two new quadruple 40 mm antiaircraft gun mounts on the foredeck are prominent. *US Navy via A. D. Baker III*

This routine was repeated for the next two days.

On December 17 the task force was ordered to rendezvous with the tankers composing Task Group 30.8. Fuel exercises began at 1029, with *Uhlman* (DD-687) refueling from *Massachusetts*. At 1319 the fueling of the destroyer was discontinued, since the 26-knot winds and heavy seas, signs of an approaching tropical storm, had caused the fueling lines to part. All fueling operations were ceased, and ComThird Fleet ordered a new fueling rendezvous for the following day at 0600, which was later changed to 0700. ComTask Group 38.1 ordered that the battleships and carriers of his force be prepared to fuel the screening destroyers in the event that the scheduled rendezvous with the tankers was not made. *Massachusetts'* deck log recorded, "From the wind and barometer indications, it appeared that the typhoon was heading for the force. The direction of the wind did not materially change during the afternoon and evening, and the barometer dropped slowly even though the track of the force was the westward, away from the storm."

The war diary entry for the next day reported a situation that continued to deteriorate, saying:

> The storm increased in intensity during the night. The barometer continued to drop slowly, and the seas continued to be heavy.

Task Group 38.1 is the southernmost of the Task Groups and therefore is farther removed from the center of the storm than either of the other groups. Even so during the morning, as the barometer continued to drop it became apparent that the storm center was not far distant.

The typhoon made it impossible to fuel from tankers, so the scheduled rendezvous was not made. Instead, the tanker group was instructed to remain in a fueling area nearby. An attempt was made about 0800 to fuel destroyers over the sterns of the carriers, but the operation was not successful and was discontinued.

By 0800 visibility was limited to a few hundred yards and the storm had increased to such proportions that some of the ships began to report personnel lost over the side and the sustaining of material damage. At 0912 Monterey reported all the planes on her hangar deck to be on fire and the loss of a gun director. Shortly thereafter she reported loss of steering control and that she was dead in the water. Her fire was brought under control at 0945, but not before the ship had sustained severe damage. Accordingly, shortly after 1000 ComTask Group 38.1 directed that McCord, Brown, Twining, Haggard and sea going tugs stand by the Monterey. This group was designated Task Unit 38.1.4. New Orleans also joined this group.

At 1030 an unidentified ship was detected by radar drifting through the formation. Avoiding action was taken, and at 1035

The battleship is viewed broadside from port while underway at a speed of 15 knots (17.6 miles per hour) off Point Wilson on July 11, 1944. The two Kingfisher planes on the catapults evidently were embarked after the previous series of July 11 photos was taken. *Naval History and Heritage Command*

Massachusetts is underway off Point Wilson. From July 10 to 15, during the first few days after modernization and repairs were completed on the ship, she was engaged in reloading stores and ammunition prior to resuming operations at sea. The ship also underwent full-power trials to verify that the power plant was operating properly. *US Navy via A. D. Baker III*

The ship is viewed from off her starboard stern while cruising off Point Wilson on July 11, 1944. During these days of checking the ship's systems and occasionally embarking provisions and ammunition, shipyard workers from Bremerton were aboard, to complete last-minute work on the ship. *US Navy via A. D. Baker III*

Massachusetts is steaming ahead at 15 knots off Point Wilson. In the days after this photo was taken, calibration work was performed on the ship's radio direction-finder and degaussing equipment, which consumed several days. After discharging navy yard workers on board at Port Angeles, Washington, on the afternoon on July 15, newly renovated *Massachusetts* departed for Pearl Harbor. *US Navy via A. D. Baker III*

a CVE, apparently dead in the water, was sighted about 500 yards off the starboard bow. An unsuccessful effort was made to communicate with the ship, later identified as Rudyard Bay, but it was soon lost from view. A warning was sent to other units in this group by Massachusetts.

Between 1000 and 1100 Boston reported losing a plane over side and Cowpens reported several planes on her hangar deck to be afire.

The barometer dropped to 29.36. It steadied at about 1100, however, and began to rise slowly.

During the afternoon the sea began to subside, visibility improved steadily, and the barometer began to rise.

ComThird Fleet directed that the Task Force rendezvous with Task Groups 30.8 and 30.7 . . . tomorrow morning at 0700 for fueling operations.

At 0815 on December 19, *Uhlman* (DD-687) again came alongside to resume the fueling operation hastily discontinued the morning of December 17. This operation was completed at 0948. At 1200, *Massachusetts* herself began receiving fuel from the tanker *Chickaskia* (AO-54), an operation that was finished at 1505.

Various messages were received during the day indicating that USS *Hull* (DD-350) capsized and sank during the typhoon,

and that USS *Spence* (DD-512), *Monaghan* (DD-354), *Waterman* (DE-740), and *Melvin R. Narvman* (DE-416) were unaccounted for. Carrier aircraft as well as destroyers initiated a search for the ships or any survivors.

While the ships most severely damaged by Typhoon Cobra were detached to return to Ulithi for repair, the remainder of Task Force 38, including *Massachusetts*, were ordered to steam toward a strike position off Luzon, to resume the strikes begun December 14. The route would take them through the area where the typhoon had hit the force, and lookouts aboard all the ships were instructed to watch for survivors. At midnight, men aboard *Baltimore* (CA-68) heard shouts from someone in the water close by, immediately after which lookouts aboard *Massachusetts* saw lights in the water off the port quarter. The destroyer *Haggard* (DD-555) was detailed to investigate.

Shortly after midnight on December 21, Halsey canceled the strike against Luzon and ordered the ships to withdraw and refuel, also ordering a search for survivors. Ultimately it was determined that *Spence* and *Monaghan*, as well as *Hull*, had been sunk by the typhoon, which also claimed 790 lives and destroyed 146 aircraft. By the end of December 21, the last of ninety-three survivors had been plucked from the sea by various ships of the task force.

Because of the large quantities of fuel that capital ships—carriers and battleships—were able to carry on board, sometimes these ships would refuel smaller ships at sea. On October 17, 1944, after assisting with the support of US carrier airstrikes on Japanese forces in Formosa (Taiwan) and just prior to joining support operations in the invasion of the Philippines, USS *Massachusetts* refueled four ships. Early on the following morning, October 17, *Massachusetts* came alongside the tanker USS *Kaskaskia* (AO-27) to take on fuel. Here, the ships are proceeding in close formation prior to passing the fuel hoses over to the battleship.

The October 18 refueling transpired on heavy seas, as is evident in this photo of crewmen on *Kaskaskia* getting drenched while handling fuel lines as *Massachusetts* maintains her course in the background. During this refueling, the battleship took on 37,553 gallons of fuel oil, and the entire procedure took just under two and a half hours.

Lines have been passed from *Kaskaskia*, right, to *Massachusetts*, with which the fuel hose is being hauled over to the battleship. According to some published sources, this refueling at sea occurred on October 17, but both *Massachusetts*' and *Kaskaskia*'s war diaries are very clear that it transpired on October 18.

A photographer aboard the carrier USS *Wasp* (CV-18) took this moody shot of *Massachusetts* as she enters the anchorage of Ulithi Atoll on November 24, 1944. The ship, along with those of Task Force 34, arrived at that base to take on ammunition and provisions after a period of combat operations in the Philippines. Subsequently, the ship would resume combat operations in the Philippines. *Naval History and Heritage Command*

With refueling complete and hope of further survivors lost, on the afternoon of December 22 Halsey ordered Task Force 38 back to Ulithi, directing that the fleet was to arrive before dark on Christmas Eve. *Massachusetts* entered the channel at Ulithi Atoll at 1400 on December 24 and dropped anchor at Berth 39 at 1438.

At 0815 on the day after Christmas, the crew mustered for a ceremony marking the change of command of Battleship Division 8, with RAdm. John Shafroth relieving RAdm. Glenn Davis. Later that day, *Massachusetts* took on 381,997 gallons of bunker fuel oil. In addition, diving operations were begun to effect repairs to the main injector valve, a process that would not be complete until December 28. On the day that the injector valve repair was completed, *Massachusetts'* Kingfisher 09665 was landing astern of the battleship when the port wing float snapped off and the aircraft overturned. Neither the pilot nor the radioman was injured, and the damaged aircraft was recovered.

The next day, both that aircraft and the one damaged by the typhoon were placed aboard lighter YSD 42, which had delivered new replacement aircraft 09596.

Having spent the past several days replenishing the ships, on December 30, *Massachusetts* and the rest of Task Group 38.1 began

making preparations to get underway. The task group consisted of the carriers USS *Yorktown*, *Wasp*, *Cabot*, and *Cowpens*; the battleships *Massachusetts* and *South Dakota*; four cruisers; and multiple destroyers. At 0713, *Massachusetts* passed the entrance buoys on her way out of the atoll and began cruising at 18 knots.

At 1207 on New Year's Eve, her lookouts spotted a yellow life raft, which upon investigation unfortunately was found to contain a lifeless body. During the morning it was found that *Massachusetts'* boilers were salting, the fault believed to a leak in the main condenser. Permission was obtained to drop out of formation and proceed independently along with escorting destroyers *Taussig* (DD-746) and *Maddox* (DD-731—the Sumner-class destroyer that would obtain great notoriety twenty years later in the Gulf of Tonkin) to the refueling point. En route, it became necessary to lock shaft 3 due to additional issues, and the mighty battleship limped along at 15 knots on three shafts.

The men of *Massachusetts* completed the repairs of the condenser at 0214 on New Year's Day, unlocked shaft 3, and began steaming toward the rendezvous with the battle line, arriving at 1430. The next day the battleship, as well as the task group, refueled, then steamed toward strike position to launch raids on Formosa.

The initial entry in *Massachusetts*' war diary for January 3, 1945, noted, "Despite squally weather and a low ceiling, carriers began launching planes for a predawn fighter sweep of target areas on Formosa at 0544." The diary noted later that

inasmuch as pilots reported extremely bad weather over the target, and as the weather continued to be squally in the vicinity of the Task Force, all strikes were cancelled shortly after noon. Only routine patrols were launched, and airborne strikes were recovered as soon as possible.

The Force returned slowly to the East during the afternoon and early evening but will return to strike the same targets tomorrow.

January 4 was a repeat of the third, with the weather over the target again being poor, and, with flight operations being difficult, strikes were canceled at noon. The task group then withdrew southeasterly for a scheduled fueling operation, which consumed the fifth.

Airstrikes against Northern Luzon resumed on January 6, and that evening the task force began steaming toward Formosa, which was to be the target on the seventh. However, as it became apparent that the weather at the target area would not be favorable, the task force was redirected so that further strikes against Northern

Luzon could be made on the seventh. Those strikes began thirty minutes before dawn and continued throughout the day. All during this time, *Massachusetts* stood at the ready to defend the task force against surface or aerial counterattack, but her guns remained silent, with no targets in sight.

After rendezvousing for refueling on the eighth, the task force steamed toward the island of Formosa, and at 0329 on January 9, screening destroyer USS *Wedderburn* (DD-684) made sound contact with an enemy sub, and USS *Twining* (DD-540) was directed to join the attack on the sub, with their orders to continue the attack until dawn, or until the submarine was sunk.

The carriers began launching strikes against Formosa just before dawn.

That evening at 2142, the task force entered the Bashi Channel, Luzon Strait, and transited to the South China Sea. After refueling, at 1724 on January 11, the task force began Operation Gratitude, a high-speed run toward Cam Ranh Bay, in hopes of catching Japanese carrier/battleship hybrids Ise and Hyuga in the harbor. At 1800, Captain Warlick addressed his crew, saying,

As you all know, we have now entered the South China Sea. This is a step of tremendous importance in advancing the war. It is of greater importance, for example, than the first raid on Truk and

Members of the crew of *Massachusetts* are attending a Roman Catholic mass on Christmas 1944. They had much to be thankful for: just one week earlier, the ship had endured a violent typhoon while at sea. The scene was on the quarterdeck, below the guns of turret 3.

Another religious service, likely Protestant, is underway on the quarterdeck of *Massachusetts*. At the time, the ship was at Urushi Anchorage, in Ulithi Atoll. Despite the Christmas holiday, the crew was busy reprovisioning the ship and conducting necessary repairs and maintenance during the time the ship was in port, from December 24 to 30. Two damaged Kingfisher floatplanes were removed from the ship, and one new one, OS2U-3, BuNo 09596, was brought aboard as a replacement.

Saipan. The reason is this: The objective of sea power is to control lines of sea communication. In the case of a power like Japan, sea communications are vital to her existence. We have previously compressed her lines of sea communication to Indies until they all passed through the South China Sea. Now we have cut those lines. They will remain cut. Our occupation of Luzon insures [*sic*] that. Japan no longer has any effective means of supplying herself from the rich resources of the Indies.

In a sense we may consider that the Navy's objective in crossing the Pacific Ocean has been to arrive at this goal. The defeat of the Japanese fleet late in October was only an incident en route, but a necessary one.

How we shall exercise control over the South China Sea will be demonstrated tomorrow. We have penetrated deep into this vital sea area without any evidence that we have been sighted as of 1600 this afternoon. Therefore, tomorrow morning we will be in a position to strike at the dense shipping which skirts the coast of Indo-China, carrying the riches of the Indies to Japan. In the next few days we shall destroy the seaborne trade of Japan from Saigon to Hong Kong. From this time henceforth, any ship that can return from the Indies to Japan will be lucky indeed.

By this move, we have not only cut the Empire in two strategically, we have also surprised the enemy tactically. We believe we will disclose a large enemy task force which is known to be in the vicinity. It will be particularly gratifying to us this task force will probably contain the battleships Ise and Hyuga, which escaped us on the morning of October 25th.

I said that there was no evidence that we had been sighted until 1600 today. Since that time, three Jakes have been knocked down to the westward. How much they saw and reported, we do not know, but there is probability that our sleep tonight will be disturbed.

But in compensation, we now have the satisfaction of seeing results of our past operations which were not easily apparent. No one could miss the significance of the defeat of the Japanese fleet in October. On the other hand, it is easy to lose sight of the importance of our repeated strikes at Luzon and Formosa. Those strikes at times seemed an endless recurring and monotonous task, but they were the means by which Task Force 38 substantially destroyed the Japanese air power in those two important bases. It is this destruction that now permits General MacArthur to occupy Luzon and for Task Force 38 finally to sever Japan's last sea communications with her Southern Empire.

The action tomorrow will involve both air and surface action. It goes without saying that, as always, we must be prepared to meet and destroy anything which the enemy may send against us.

At dawn on January 12, Task Force 38 launched airstrikes against Saigon and Cam Ranh Bay, and Task Group 34.5, a special surface-striking group comprising the fast battleships, was formed and dispatched toward the harbors. Alas, the aviators reported that *Ise* and *Hyuga* were not to be seen, and Task Group 34.5 was recalled and disbanded, with the battleships, including *Massachusetts*, returning to their previous task groups.

The task force's aircraft, however, were notably effective, finding three Japanese convoys at sea and, during the subsequent attacks, sinking four cargo ships, seven badly needed tankers, and nine escort vessels. Further ships were sank in port before the task force began to retire on a northeasterly course. En route on the fifteenth and sixteenth, planes from the carriers launched attacks against Hong Kong, Amoy, and the Swatow area of the China coast, as well as Formosa.

Heavy seas forced the abortion of refueling efforts on the seventeenth, and on the eighteenth the task force was ordered toward Luzon in hopes of finding a lee in which refueling could be resumed. This was successful, and refueling destroyers was resumed while steaming south. On the nineteenth, *Massachusetts* herself refueled from the T-2 fleet oiler *Neosho* (AO-48). Multiple radar contacts with unidentified aircraft throughout the day culminated for the men of *Massachusetts* at 1915, when a Japanese aircraft was spotted approaching the starboard bow at low angle, causing the battlewagon to open fire with the 5-inch, 40 mm, and 20 mm batteries—her first shots fired in anger in 1945. The results of her AA gunners' fury were undetermined. At 2000 she began leaving the South China Sea through the Balintang Channel, Luzon Strait, on an easterly course.

Thirty minutes before sunrise on January 22, the carriers of the task force began launching airstrikes against targets on Okinawa as the force passed in the vicinity. The next day the force rendezvoused with tankers for fueling, and upon completion the newly formed Task Group 38.6, including *New Jersey, Boston, Baltimore, Hancock*, and *Langley* and some escorts, was detached and proceeded to Ulithi. Later in the day, the balance of the task force was ordered to Ulithi, to arrive before noon on the twenty-sixth.

At 0700 on January 24, RAdm. Sherman, temporary commander of Task Force 38, ordered the formation of Task Force 34, which would include Battleship Division 8, of which *Massachusetts* was flagship. The rest of TF 34, under command of RAdm. Shafroth, consisted of *South Dakota, Wisconsin, Washington, North Carolina, Pasadena, Astoria, Wilkes-Barre, Vincennes, Miami, Biloxi*, and two destroyer divisions. On the next day the battle line conducted tactical exercises and training drills. On January 26, *South Dakota* and *Wisconsin* formed on *Massachusetts* at dawn for main and secondary battery firing, which was completed at 0909, after which Task Force 34 proceeded to Ulithi, with *Massachusetts* entering Mugai Channel on 1307, dropping anchor at Berth 5.

Massachusetts remained anchored in Ulithi, with the crew enjoying some time on the beaches and the ship being reprovisioned until February 10, when preparations began to be made to get underway. She sortied from the harbor at 1024 as a unit of Task Group 58.1 to support airstrikes on Tokyo, Okinawa, Iwo Jima, and Chichi Jima, all in support of the landings on Iwo Jima. In the afternoon, at sea, main battery-firing exercises were conducted. At 1805, while recovering the aircraft, *Massachusetts'* plane 09596 overturned upon landing. The aircraft crew was rescued by USS *Murray* (DD-576), which then shelled the damaged aircraft in order to sink it.

On St. Valentine's Day, Capt. Warlick addressed his crew:

For the last six months we have been engaged in operations in support of the Philippines campaign. For us that campaign seems to be finished. It now falls to General MacArthur's forces, including the Seventh Fleet, to carry that campaign to its completion. The Seventh Fleet now does not include the battleships and many of the cruisers and other light forces which took part in the Philippines campaign. Those ships are properly a part of the Central Pacific Force and have now returned to the operational command of Adm. Nimitz and form a part of the Fifth Fleet.

We are beginning the first operation of a new campaign, in Task Force 58 of the Fifth Fleet. This Fifth Fleet is under the command of Admiral Spruance. It is composed of a number of task forces which follow the organization to which we have been accustomed. That is, an amphibious force, under the old master, Vice Admiral Kelly Turner; the support farce, composed of the old battleships plus cruisers and destroyers, under Rear Admiral B. J. Rogers; and Task Force 58, acting as covering force under the command of the veteran Vice Admiral Mitscher. As usual, there will be a landing. We are now en route to our usual task of paving the way. Where the landing will be will become clear in a few days. More important to us is the part we are to play. It is clear to all that our next landing must be close to the Japanese homeland. It follows that the objective of Task Force 58 must be even closer. Until the present time, each of our objectives have appeared to be more important that the previous ones. In each one we expected to encounter stiff opposition. In most of these cases our expectations have not been fulfilled by the Japanese. However, on our present mission we propose to find out what he can do in what we presume to be his strongest positions. In short, the objective of Task Force 58 is the Tokyo area.

In this area the enemy can be presumed to have strong air forces. Close by, we can presume he has what remains of his fleet, which approximates two of our task groups.

USS *Massachusetts*, foreground, is proceeding with Task Group 58.1 while conducting gunnery and tactical exercises on February 12, 1945. The group, including two aircraft carriers visible on the horizon, were en route to Japan, where the group would conduct a series of strikes in support of the Iwo Jima landings a week later.

On our side, Task Force 58 is stronger than it ever has been before. Our Task Force Admiral and Task Group Admirals are the most experienced in the whole Navy. Our Group Commander is Rear Admiral J. J. Clark. This Group has been chosen by Vice Admiral Mitscher for the position of honor on the Advanced Flank. We will be the closest to Tokyo.

There is a good chance that we can achieve strategic surprise. That we can achieve tactical surprise is too much to expect. Whether we do or not we must expect strong air opposition, because this time we are adding insult to injury. This time the Jap will be fighting for his sacred homeland, for which he can be expected to fight with more than his usual fanatical zeal.

The strike begins at dawn 16 February, day after tomorrow, and will last one to three days, depending on the circumstances. During this time, we must be more on the alert than ever before. We must overcome any tendencies we may have to a sense of safety as judged from past experience. The anti-aircraft gunners on watch must play an alert, "heads up," game, and be ready to shoot instantly and hit. If the weather is bad, which we expect, the time for shooting will be too short to be effective otherwise. If Task Force 58 finds worthy air opposition at Tokyo, we can expect a hard fight, in which only our own skill and alertness can protect the carriers and ourselves from enemy attackers which get through our fighters.

The whole Task Group is looking to our anti-aircraft gunners to down any Jap plane that comes within range of their guns. The gunners are looking to the radarmen, the lookouts, and CIC to assist them, but, finally, the men at the guns and the directors must rely upon themselves to have their guns on every Jap plane in sight before he can strike. If Task Force 58 can destroy a substantial part of the enemy's air forces and aircraft factories around Tokyo, the next phase of this war can be pointed much more directly at Tokyo than would otherwise be possible. Such a project deserves and must have nothing less than the utmost effort of each of us. To this end, check your battle station and your equipment to see that all is in order. Leave nothing to be done at the last minute and leave nothing to chance.

Indeed, at 0648 the carriers of Task Force 58 began launching predawn sweeps of Japanese airfields near Tokyo and Yokohama. These were followed by dive and horizontal bomber strikes against those targets.

That morning as well, *Massachusetts* radar made a surface contact at 15,000 yards, and *Haynsworth* (DD-700) was detailed to investigate. The surface contact was revealed to be patrol craft 36, Nanshin Maru, which was sunk by Haynsworth, which then

Massachusetts is being refueled at sea by the fleet oiler USS *Saugatuck* (AO-75). Although some published sources indicate that the photo was taken on April 20, 1945, the ship's war diary makes no mention of this refueling on or around that date. Instead, the war diary indicates that *Massachusetts* was refueled by USS *Kaskaskia* both on April 17 and 22. The only mention in the war diary of a refueling of *Massachusetts* by *Saugatuck* anytime near April 20 was on March 22, 1945, when the battleship took on 656,631 gallons of fuel from the fleet oiler.

Little is known of this photo of USS *Massachusetts* with her secondary gun batteries firing ferociously. It possibly was taken during the Okinawa campaign in the spring of 1945. To the upper right are several antiaircraft shell bursts and a single aircraft.

turned her attention to the auxiliary submarine chaser Wafu Maru, acting as a picket boat. After sinking that vessel as well, the US destroyer rescued eleven survivors.

Although enemy aircraft were reported about 1000, and picket destroyers were seen firing about 25,000 yards away, *Massachusetts'* war diary notes, "No enemy aircraft approached this ship, and we did not open fire."

The next day, February 17, the airstrikes were repeated, although weather over the targets limited visibility. At 1731 the task force began retiring to the south at 21 knots, and at 0800 the next morning the ships turned into the wind and the carriers launched strikes against Chichi Jima, a large island about 150 miles north of Iwo Jima. Those strikes continued throughout the day.

February 19 was filled with refueling, with *Massachusetts* taking on 593,252 gallons of fuel, and gunnery exercises for the 5-inch and machine gun batteries. This was in preparation for the attack on Iwo Jima, which began the next day. *Massachusetts'* war diary entry for February 20 reads simply and completely, "Operating in area of Iwo Jima. At dawn carriers began launching strikes as direct air support of the landings effected on Iwo Jima. Operations continued throughout the day."

Massachusetts did not fire at the beaches; instead, she provided antiaircraft defense for the carriers. The preinvasion bombardment, which lasted three days rather than the ten days that the Marines requested, was carried out by the older, slower battleships USS *Arkansas* (BB-33), New York (BB-34), Texas (BB-35), *Nevada* (BB-36), *Idaho* (BB-42), and *Tennessee* (BB-34), as well as five cruisers. On the nineteenth the bombardment effort was joined by *North Carolina* (BB-55), *Washington* (BB-56), and *West Virginia* (BB-48) and three more cruisers.

Massachusetts remained on station with the carriers, which continued to launch strikes against Iwo Jima through February 21. The twenty-second found the carrier aircraft conducting routine patrols as the fleet prepared to rendezvous for refueling, which happened on the twenty-third. When the refueling was complete, with *Massachusetts* alone taking on 279,755 gallons, the task force steamed again toward Tokyo, near which, on the twenty-fifth, carrier airstrikes were launched against airfields, aircraft, and aircraft engine plants in the Tokyo area.

However, heavy snow made air operations over the target area difficult, and the last strike of the day was launched just after noon. Since the weather forecast for the following day was also bleak, the task force was shifted to target Kobe. As the new target was being approached, heavy seas and bad weather were encountered, and the decision was made to retire to the south.

The twenty-seventh and part of the twenty-eighth were spent refueling, and on March 1, airstrikes were launched against Okinawa. At 1351, *Massachusetts* catapulted both her Kingfishers after receiving a call concerning a US flier down in the water off southwestern Okinawa. Unfortunately, they were not able to locate the pilot; however, while returning to *Massachusetts*, Kingfisher pilot Lt. G. A. Robinson intercepted a message that a Bennington (CV-20) pilot was down off southeastern Okinawa. Robinson was able to locate and rescue that VF-82 pilot, Ens. William F. Hahn, and return with him. The following day, the destroyer *McKee* (DD-575) came alongside to pick up Hahn via breeches buoy and return him to Bennington.

On the morning of March 3, *Massachusetts* and Task Unit 58.1 rendezvoused with the fueling group, and Sigsbee (DD-502) came alongside to transfer a patient for medical treatment, *Massachusetts* having much-larger medical facilities and staff than did most other ships in the fleet.

Just after noon on March 3, *Massachusetts* was detached from Task Unit 58.1 and, along with Battleship Divisions 6, 7, and 8 (*Massachusetts* and *Indiana* composed BatDiv 8) and Cruiser Divisions 13, 14, and 17, and their escorts, became Task Force 59.

Main- and secondary-battery firing exercises were conducted by Task Force 59 during March 4 and the morning of March 5. At 1155, Ulithi Atoll was sighted, and at 1420 *Massachusetts* anchored in Berth B-1, an antiaircraft firing anchorage.

At 0713 on March 7, the gate in the socket of the gangway davit failed, causing the davit to fall on Seaman First Class James Zelmon Dyess, fatally injuring him. The crew assembled aft at 0850 on March 8 for funeral services for Dyess, who was later interred at the National Memorial Cemetery of the Pacific.

As the fleet was at rest at Ulithi on March 11, men on *Massachusetts* saw a twin-engine kamikaze P1Y1 "Frances" plunge into the starboard aft just below the flight deck of *Randolph* (CV-15). Soon, flames could be seen rising from the carrier, which was moored nearby. This was a part of a Japanese long-range kamikaze mission, code name Tan No. 2. Only two of the twenty-four Franceses that were launched from Kyushu, each carrying a 1,700-pound bomb, reached Ulithi. One struck USS *Randolph*, causing extensive damage, and the men of *Massachusetts* saw the second one crash onto a road on the small island of Sorlen after missing a nearby ship.

Shortly before noon on March 14, Task Force 59, including *Massachusetts*, got underway from Ulithi. As compared to its previous composition, the task force now included Cruiser Divisions 10 and 16 but did not include Cruiser Division 13.

After spending the next day conducting gunnery and radar-tracking exercises, the ships rejoined Task Force 58 as the armada steamed toward Kyushu.

In the early hours of March 18, Japanese aircraft dropped what *Massachusetts'* war diary described as "a well-placed pattern of flares approximately 4,500 yards from the formation." Six minutes later, at 0502, the air attack alarm was sounded, and three minutes after that, *Massachusetts'* 5-inch guns began firing, with the 40 mm guns following suit moments later. At 0513 a Japanese plane passed over *Massachusetts* at an extremely low altitude. Big Mamie's antiaircraft batteries stayed busy throughout the day, her war diary noting that

single planes continued to attack ships in the formation. A second plane was taken under fire by many ships of this group, burst into flames, and crashed into the water . . . 5,000 yards from this ship.

At 0604 a "Nell" crossed our stern heading toward *Wasp*. The plane was taken under fire by our machine gun battery[,] and a fire was observed in the starboard engine. The plane continued to close . . . executed a "wing over" and crashed in the water. . . . It is thought that hits were obtained on this plane by our machine gun battery.

At 0725 an enemy plane dove out of the clouds just ahead of this ship, apparently trying to bomb or dive into *Hornet*. Our machine gun batteries opened fire immediately, hitting the plane, which crashed into the water near the *Hornet*.

An enemy plane diving on one of our carriers was taken under fire by our machine gun battery, at 1311. The plane crashed in flames close to the starboard side of the *Hornet*. It is believed that this plane was destroyed by our machine gun battery.

Opened fire at 2227 with secondary battery. One of the enemy planes was observed to burst into flames and crash into the water off our port quarter, range about 8,000 yards.

As the air battle was unfolding over the task force, the carriers were launching strikes against Japanese airfields and installations. Those strikes continued on the nineteenth as well, with Japanese airfields, shore installations, and shipping in southern Kyushu and Shikoku feeling the wrath of the task force's aviators.

Simultaneously, the Japanese continued to lash out at the carriers, with USS *Wasp* being hit by a bomb and suffering minimal damage. *Franklin* was not as lucky; being heavily battered and ravaged by fire, she was taken under tow by *Pittsburgh*. *Pittsburgh* could make only 6 knots while withdrawing with the carrier in tow; however, the entire task group withdrew with the struggling pair, offering considerable protection. The next day the speed of the task group increased as *Franklin*'s men were able to restore two screws to operation and cast off the tow line.

On March 21, as the ships continued to retire from Kyushu, *Massachusetts* executed an ordered turn, during which a large wave broke over the stern of the battleship, knocking the Kingfisher on the port catapult to the deck, damaging it to such an extent that the ship's crew could not repair the aircraft. Also, on the twenty-first, all the damaged ships were transferred to Task Group 58.2, which was to steam to Ulithi.

The remaining task force refueled on the twenty-second, and also that day, the flagship of the refueling force, the light cruiser *Detroit* (CL-8), transferred her Kingfisher 09676 to *Massachusetts* to replace the one damaged the day before.

The carrier aircraft were back in action at dawn on March 23, launching strikes against Okinawa; the biggest excitement for *Massachusetts* was maneuvering to avoid a mine that passed close aboard to port. The next day would be very different.

At 0455 on March 24, units began maneuvering to form Task Group 59.7, consisting of Battleship Divisions 6, 7, and 8. *Massachusetts* was assigned to the Southern Group, 59.7.3, tasked with covering the minesweeping group working close inshore, and then following the minesweepers into the swept area in order to close range on the enemy.

With the range to the target closed to 23,000 yards, *Massachusetts'* main battery roared at 0943, and the first salvo landed 200 yards over. By 0951, she had closed range to 20,500 yards and was hitting her target with the third salvo. *Massachusetts* remained on the firing line for three hours, at which time she withdrew in order to recover her aircraft. During recovery at 1257, the main float of O2SU-3 Kingfisher 5483 collapsed, causing the plane to nose over. While the aircraft had to be sunk by gunfire, thankfully the pilot and radioman were rescued. At 1337, *Massachusetts* rejoined the firing line, and at 1343 she resumed her bombardment. At 1415 she ceased firing, having expended 180 rounds of 16-inch/45-caliber ammunition during the day.

March 25 found *Massachusetts* serving as a floating antiaircraft battery protecting the carriers, which were again launching airstrikes against Okinawa. At the end of the day, she retired toward a refueling area, where she took on 489,707 gallons of bunker fuel on the morning of the twenty-sixth.

March 27 found *Massachusetts* off Okinawa launching strikes against positions on Amami Oshima, the largest island between Kyushu and Okinawa. Reports from the naval aviators stated that opposition from the island was negligible. But for firing the starboard 5-inch mounts on approaching aircraft at 0641, the day was quiet for the men of USS *Massachusetts*.

In the last few months of the war in the Pacific, Allied forces mounted a naval bombardment campaign against industrial and military facilities in the coastal areas of the Japanese home islands, largely in hopes of luring enemy aircraft into attacking the ships so that the Allies could reduce that threat in advance of the planned invasion of Japan. The first such raid, against the steelworks/ironworks at Kamaishi, in the northern part of the island of Honshu, was prosecuted by Task Unit 38.1. This photo, taken from USS *South Dakota* (BB-57), shows TU 38.1 underway, with USS *Indiana* (BB-58) followed by *Massachusetts* and the cruisers USS *Chicago* (CA-136) and USS *Quincy* (CA-71). Task Unit 38.1 began the first naval bombardment of the iron-and-steel plant at Kamaishi on the morning of July 14. *Massachusetts* expended three hundred rounds of 16-inch high-capacity ammunition during the bombardment, and the raid caused severe damage to the plant. *Naval History and Heritage Command*

However, the men of Task Group 58.1 received somewhat jarring news at 1100 on March 28. The war diary records the situation like this:

A message was received from the Task Group Commander indicating the Group was heading North to intercept the Japanese Fleet. Amplifying reports indicated we expected to strike the enemy fleet as it sortied from Bungo Suido[,] and plans were made to detach the support units of Task Group 58.1 and allow them to proceed Northward to destroy any cripples remaining afloat after our air strikes had been completed.

As the day wore on, however, that plan began to unravel, the war diary noting that

at 1430 a search and attack group was launched. At 1500 a group of 40 fighters was launched to sweep airfields on Southern Kyushu before proceeding to attack the Japanese Fleet.

Unfortunately the enemy fleet units were never located, and our planes were forced to release their bombs on targets of opportunity along the southeast coast. Carriers recovered aircraft shortly after dark.

Thus, the veteran main battery gunners of *Massachusetts* lost another chance to do exactly what the ship was designed to do—face off against other men of war. Thus, on the twenty-ninth, rather than engaging Japanese surface ships with her big rifles, *Massachusetts* was off southern Kyushu acting as a massive floating antiaircraft battery, but even with that, no enemy was spotted and thus not a shot was fired. After a pause on the thirtieth to refuel, the last day of March was a repeat of the twenty-ninth.

On April 1, the Marines began going ashore on Okinawa, while *Massachusetts* and the rest of TF58 steamed offshore, the carriers providing air cover, and the battlewagons providing antiaircraft cover for the carriers. In fact, on April 2, BB-59's 5-inch guns fired at an enemy aircraft for the first time in several days. The target of the task group's aircraft shifted to enemy positions on the nearby island of Sakishima Gunto on April 3, and then refueling the next day, after which they returned to positions off Okinawa. After refueling on the fourth, the men of *Massachusetts* locked shafts 2 and 4 in order to repair a leak in a condenser.

Off Okinawa on April 6, *Massachusetts*' 20 mm and 40 mm guns fired on multiple Japanese planes attacking other ships of the task force, scoring several hits and likely accounting for the downing of two aircraft.

During a bombardment, the navigator of USS *Missouri* is using a pelorus on the starboard side of the navigating bridge to fix the position of the ship. The pelorus features a rotating sight on the center of a compass scale, with which relative bearings may be taken.

On April 7, word was received that major units of the Japanese fleet, including Yamato, had sortied from Bungo Suido. The intent was to beach Yamato, the world's largest battleship, on Okinawa and use her as a shore battery. Further reconnaissance reported that the massive battleship had in her company two light cruisers and eight destroyers (in reality, there was only one light cruiser—*Yahagi*—and eight destroyers in the company of *Yamato*). Task Force 58 launched 380 aircraft to attack the Japanese ships and succeeded in sinking *Yamato* and several of her escorts. *Massachusetts* got word of the aviators' successes at about 1600. Earlier that afternoon, at about 1541, a Japanese aircraft dove out of the clouds of the task group and was taken under fire by *Massachusetts* and other ships of the task group, which collectively were able to shoot the enemy down before it could press home an attack.

On April 8, *Massachusetts* not only refueled at sea but also took on fourteen 16-inch rounds as well as 440 5-inch projectiles and seventy cans of 40 mm before resuming her position east of Okinawa.

She refueled again on April 11 and was back on station off Okinawa on April 12. On that day, her AA gunners engaged a pair of Japanese suicide aircraft that appeared to be targeting *Indiana*. Fortunately, both aircraft were downed by alert AA gunners of the ships in the task group.

On the thirteenth, Kingfisher 5595, piloted by Lt. Robinson, was involved in the recovery of yet another downed Allied pilot.

On the fourteenth, the group came under attack yet again, and as a result two enemy aircraft were downed in the early afternoon by AA gunners, with one coming down to port of *Indiana* and the other astern of *Bennington*. Late in the night of the fifteenth, unidentified aircraft were detected 49 miles out. Destroyers of the picket line opened fire, and *Taussig* reported downing one of the interlopers at 2307.

At 1201 the next day, an enemy aircraft dove on *San Jacinto* (CVL-30) and *Massachusetts*' antiaircraft battery opened fire, as did those of other screening vessels. The aircraft attempted to flee but was downed by the barrage. Two hours later, an aircraft dove on *Massachusetts* herself but was downed by the combat air patrol, with the enemy crashing about 6,000 yards from the battleship.

Underway replenishment on April 17 put 926,252 gallons of bunker fuel in *Massachusetts*' tanks, along with 58 16-inch rounds, 532 5-inch rounds, 3,232 40 mm rounds, and 600 cans of 5-inch powder in her magazines. Also, Kingfisher 5959 was brought aboard as a replacement. After this reprovisioning, *Massachusetts* returned to her station off Okinawa, where she had an uneventful nine-day period, interrupted only by another refueling on the twenty-second.

On April 26, *Massachusetts* again topped off her tanks, and the next day at 1849 she and the rest of the task force began to retire to Ulithi, arriving there on April 30.

The first eight days of May 1945 were spent at anchor at Ulithi largely provisioning the ship, with the final two days spent at anchor conducting antiaircraft gunnery exercises. The war diary for *Massachusetts* on May Day notes, "At 1000 transferred one 'dud' aircraft, #5595, to Fallalop Island." The next day the crew assembled forward for a change-of-command ceremony, during which Capt. John Redman relieved Capt. Warlick as CO of *Massachusetts*.

At 0659 on May 9, she was underway as part of Task Unit 58.1.5, conducting gunnery, radar, and tactical exercises prior to joining the carriers of Task Group 58.1 at 1745 on May 11. During the tactical exercises prior to the rendezvous, both of *Massachusetts'* aircraft were damaged on their catapults by bursting ordnance, rendering them temporarily inoperative.

While speaking to the crew over public address on May 12, Capt. Redman made them aware of a new enemy weapon, saying in part,

Today we joined with 58.3 and under VAdm. Mitscher are again ready for business. This morning, we fueled in the area just east of Okinawa and are now headed for a strike position off Kyushu. Commencing tomorrow morning, Adm. Mitscher intends to give the airfields and facilities there a good working over, and may turn the aviators loose again on what is left of the Jap fleet in the Inland Sea. The Japs have not been accepting their destruction with very good grace recently as you all know. In addition to the kamikaze attack, we now have to watch out for Baka bombs with their suicide pilots. These bombs, so far, have generally been launched by Bettys. Like everything else the Japs produce, the Baka bombs can be shot down. However, it should be known that they are painted a silver color, are hard to detect[,] and travel about 400 miles per hour. We may expect them to send these as well as everything else they can operate out against us.

In the early-morning hours of May 13, as the Task Unit was approaching strike position, reports of unidentified aircraft approaching the formation called the men of *Massachusetts* to be roused to their air attack stations at 0146. The ship was secured from air attack at 0405, and at dawn the carriers began launching their strikes against Kyushu. Air attack stations were manned again at 2133 and were subsequently secured from same at 2320.

The early morning of May 14 was very much a repeat of the morning before, with air attack stations being called at 0132. However, none of the enemy planes came within gun range, and the ship was secured from air attack at 0226. Air attack was called again at 0330, with the war diary recording, "Several ships of the group fired at enemy planes and at 0423 an enemy plane was shot down." At 0516 the ship was secured from air attack, only for the men to have to return to their stations at 0625 as several Japanese planes evaded the combat air patrol to attack the ships. Two aircraft were downed in quick succession, one at 0705 and the other two minutes later; finally, *Massachusetts* was secured from air attack once again at 0855.

In the last days of World War II, Allied forces returned to Kamaishi to continue the bombardment of the ironworks/steelworks. The attacking force was Task Unit 34.8.1, which contained the same ships that bombarded Kamaishi in July as well as several more USN, Royal Navy, and Royal New Zealand Navy Ships. A photographer aboard USS *Indiana* took this photo of USS *Massachusetts* firing a salvo at Kamaishi on the afternoon of August 9, 1945. This attack caused much more damage to the plant and ancillary facilities than the July 14 bombardment. On the same date, Nagasaki was the target of the second atomic bomb attack, and Emperor Hirohito would announce the surrender of Japan six days later.

An aerial reconnaissance photograph, as published in *Massachusetts'* wartime cruise book, shows the Kamaishi ironworks/steelworks. The furnaces are to the right, with the numerous chimneys faintly visible.

Smoke billows from the Kamaishi iron-and-steel plant during a naval bombardment. To the upper right is Kamaishi Harbor; the view is toward the east. During this second naval bombardment of Kamaishi, the 16-inch guns of *Massachusetts* fired a total of 165 rounds. Following the war, the US Strategic Bombing Survey devoted a full volume to a report on the devastation wreaked on Kamaishi in the July 14 and August 9, 1945, naval bombardments.

The task unit remained in strike position for several days. On May 16, *Massachusetts* launched Kingfisher 5959 to accompany a fighter strike on Minami Daito Shima, in an effort to be nearby should a flier be downed. This proved to be fortuitous, since Lt. Cenedelia, in 5959, was to rescue Lt. Cmdr. Hessel of USS *Bennington*, who was shot down during the strike.

But for periodic refueling, *Massachusetts* remained on station, and her guns silent but for training, through May 26.

At midnight on May 28, VAdm. Spruance hauled down his flag and Admiral Halsey raised his; thereby the Fifth Fleet became the Third Fleet, and *Massachusetts'* task group became 38.1 rather than 58.1. Operationally, the task group began operating south of Okinawa on May 29, taking this position to support ground operations on the island, moving away on May 31 for refueling, and again steaming toward Okinawa on June 1.

During the morning watch on June 3, *Massachusetts* refueled three destroyers, and just before midnight Task Group 38.1 began retiring southward for a scheduled fueling rendezvous. *Massachusetts* began taking on fuel at 0820 on June 4. An hour and ten minutes later, the task group was ordered to cease fueling operations and "retire on 110° (T) at best possible speed" in order to avoid a typhoon that was reported to be southwest of the force. The task group formed up and began making 12 knots. Perhaps as a result of the lessons learned during the previous typhoon, during which lightly laden destroyers had capsized, at 1102 the heavy ships were ordered to refuel any destroyers that had not been refueled from tankers. As a result, *Massachusetts* refueled Schroeder (DD-501), completing the operation at 1139. By 1200 the speed had increased to 14 knots, and Task Group 30.8, the logistics group, was retiring with the combat ships. About 1500, *San Juan* (CL-54) and *Belleau Wood* (CVL-24) were sent to the fueling group for refueling, returning to 38.1 at 1820.

Massachusetts' war diary for June 4–5 includes many remarks about the weather, reading,

During the day, from noon until dark, weather was intermittently bad with occasional squalls accompanied by high winds and heavy rain.

By 0100, 5 June 1945, the barometer had dropped to 29.42. The wind was force 7, causing a heavy swell. From 0100 until shortly before 0700 the force of the storm increased. . . . At about 0630 the wind increased to an estimated 100 knots. A number of ships reported having serious difficulty, Pittsburg losing her bow and Duluth having her bow buckled.

At approximately 0700 this ship passed through the "eye" of the typhoon. The barometer dropped to 28.30, the wind dropped to 26 knots[,] and the visibility increased from a few hundred feet to about 10,000 yards. The ceiling rose from zero to an estimated 5,000 feet[,] and the circular structure of the typhoon was clearly discernable [*sic*]. Seas in the typhoon's eye were mountainous, being much greater even than those encountered when the wind was estimated at 100 knots.

After the ship passed through the "eye" of the storm, the winds and seas began to subside and the barometer rose steadily.

Massachusetts suffered only minor damage from the storm, the principal casualty being the destruction of one of our Kingfishers, which was damaged beyond repair.

Yet again, Halsey had steamed his ships into the path of a typhoon, in this case Typhoon Connie, sometimes referred to as Typhoon Viper, perhaps an homage to the previous Typhoon Cobra, which had been so devastating to Task Force 38.

The Third Fleet report on this typhoon reads in part,

On 3 June 1945 a tropical disturbance was reported East of the Philippines and there began a most unfortunate series of events which culminated in extensive storm damage to many ships of the THIRD Fleet. Initial reports varied widely as to the character, locale, course, and speed of the reported disturbance. The different position reports covered an area of about 34,000 miles; with dangerous water and enemy territory to the North and West, Commander THIRD Fleet was compelled to move TF 38 and TG 30.8 to the eastward to gain sea room in which he could later maneuver to safety. Confused reports and serious communication delays deprived Commander THIRD Fleet and other commanders of accurate and timely information, and the aerologists, including the Weather Central, Guam, were at odds with each other and much confused. Although Commander THIRD Fleet extricated TG 38.4 without damage, the ships of TG 38.1 and 30.8 took a severe buffeting with resulting storm damage as listed in Enclosure (E).

Commander THIRD Fleet has made strong representations in the past, including recommendation in his top[-]secret serial 0085 of 26 January 1945, for the establishment of aircraft weather reconnaissance squadrons composed of long-range aircraft. He again emphasized the absolute necessity of improved typhoon[-] warning communications and typhoon reconnaissance and tracking by long-range aircraft, preferably B-29's. Those recommendations are repeated here, and Commander THIRD Fleet will continue to repeat them until a satisfactory typhoon[-] warning service is established; and until then the Fleet will be in constant jeopardy from these vicious and unpredictable storms. On 10 June CinCPac instituted typhoon advisory dispatches, transmitting in plain language with "URGENT" precedence, and on 12 June 1945 word was received that B-29's

were to be used for reconnaissance. These two steps will do much to reduce typhoon hazards inasmuch as B-29's can actually fly over the storm center, track[,] and make "eye" witness reports. One further step is needed and recommended: The amalgamation of POA and SWPA weather services into a single Western Pacific Weather Service.

After passage of the storm, Commander THIRD Fleet reported to CinCPac that in spite of damage[,] all forces were ready to carry out assigned tasks, and planes were immediately made to resume attacks against Kyushu to test the newly-devised [*sic*] attack plan and to support the Okinawa operations. On 8 June 1945 from a position about 250 miles South, Southeast of Kyushu, TG's 38.1 and 38.4 launched about 200 fighters and fighter bombers for a concentrated attack against the Kanoya fields where previous visual and photographic reconnaissance had shown a big concentration.

By June 7, Task Group 38.1 had re-formed and was again operating off Okinawa, furnishing air support for troops on the ground. That day, the men of *Massachusetts* jettisoned the hulk of typhoon-damaged Kingfisher 09676, after having stripped the airframe of usable equipment. The next morning, the aircraft of the task group conducted a raid against airfields and aircraft on Kyushu.

At dawn on June 9, the task group rendezvoused with the fueling group and, that afternoon, launched airstrikes against Minami Daito Jima and Okino Daito Jima.

On June 10, *Massachusetts* was able to employ her main battery, as the ship, detailed to Task Group 30.2 (BatDiv 8 and DesDiv 121), bombarded targets on Minami Daito Jima from 0620 to 0724 with her 16-inch rifles. After the big guns stopped firing, the secondary battery fired on shore installations, continuing until 0800. *Massachusetts'* main battery had fired fifteen salvos, expending eighty-one rounds, while the 5-inch mounts fired one hundred rounds at various targets.

Following the bombardment, *Massachusetts* and her consorts steamed toward San Pedro Bay, Leyte Gulf, Philippine Islands, anchoring there at 1638 on June 13.

Big Mamie remained in San Pedro Bay until July 1, when she steamed north toward Tokyo as a unit of Support Unit 1. During the morning of July 9, the force began to encounter a number of floating mines, with Maddox destroying one 3,000 yards off *Massachusetts'* bow at 0809.

At 1800, Capt. Redman addressed the crew, saying in part,

You have noted that the Okinawa operation has been considered concluded. Although some mopping up may be going on, Okinawa no longer requires direct support of the fast carrier task force, i.e.[,] Task Force 38[,] of which we are a part. Further amphibious operations are undoubtedly being planned by High Command and will take place as soon as everything is ready.

Okinawa has assumed the role of an offensive base and you will hear more and more of air operations from that location. The B-29s you read of daily in the press. Their numbers will increase and they will be joined by B-32s[,] whose performance and bomb load is comparable to the B-29.

Task Force 38 is stronger than ever at this time. We have three groups each containing 5 carriers. We have a total of 8 fast battleships[,] many new cruisers[,] and a much more comfortable number of destroyers than last time.

Tomorrow morning at dawn from waters east of Tokyo we will send many air strikes against the area. We hope it will be a surprise. There are a good part of the Jap airfields in the Tokyo area[,] and they probably contain many of their aircraft. There may be a violent reaction to our visit. It is our job to take care of any that get by the aircraft patrols. Our own task group 38.1 has the honorary seat again on the western side nearest Tokyo.

In a day or so if all goes well[,] the battleships have an interesting assignment. BatDiv 8 and a heavy cruiser will go well up north and bombard shore installations on the island of Hokkaido. Carrier aircraft will cover us. This will take us into waters which may contain anchored mines and possibly close enough for enemy shore battery fire. We will use full charge 16.

I know you would like to some word about the probable time of our departure for the Navy Yard. There has been nothing official. I feel certain that in the normal course of events we will be the next fast battleship to go back. Many factors influence the actual date[,] and the decision to send us some of them being, the desire to keep as many as possible in the operational area, the workload of the Navy Yard, and the desire to keep these ships in a good state [of] repair.

My best guess is that unless something happens to one of the other fast battleships, we will start our trip home some time in the first ten days of August.

As it would turn out, Capt. Redman was mistaken. The following morning, aircraft from the carriers attacked the

In an undated photograph, there has been a pause in firing by several of the twin 5-inch/38-caliber gun mounts on USS *Massachusetts*. Spent powder cases are carpeting the deck. On the front shields of the gun mounts to the sides of the gun barrels are curved frames associated with the blast bags, also called bloomers. Reportedly, *Massachusetts* was the only ship in her class to have these frames on the 5-inch gun mounts.

Honshu area, after which the force withdrew in order to rendezvous with the tanker at dawn the next morning. At 0155 on July 12, *South Dakota*, *San Juan*, and *John Rodgers* (DD-574) all reported sighting torpedo tracks. The task group took evasive action, but the screening destroyers were unable to make sonar contact with a submarine. The refueling took place as scheduled beginning at dawn, after which the group steamed again toward Honshu.

Adverse weather on July 13 prevented the launching of the scheduled airstrikes against Honshu and Hokkaido. Those strikes were instead conducted on July 14. More significant for the men of *Massachusetts*, Task Unit 34.8.1 was detached from Task Force 38.1. This task unit consisted of *Massachusetts*, *South Dakota*, and *Indiana* plus cruisers *Chicago* and *Quincy*, as well as escorting destroyers. This force was to bombard Kamaishi on the Japanese mainland island of Honshu. At 0842 the Japanese mainland was sighted by *Massachusetts*' lookouts. At 1016, General Quarters was sounded as *Massachusetts* prepared to shell the Imperial Iron and Steel Works at Kamaishi. *Massachusetts*' main battery opened fire at 1213 and ceased firing at 1409 after expending three hundred rounds of high-capacity ammunition, thereafter rejoining Task Group 38.1 at 2120.

The next day the aircraft resumed their attacks on targets in Honshu and Hokkaido, and on the sixteenth the task group withdrew to a refueling point. The task group was back in strike position on the seventeenth, with the strikes resuming at dawn. Fog began to close in around noon, and as a result the afternoon strikes were canceled. Strikes resumed at dawn on the eighteenth, and that same morning two floating mines were spotted nearby, evidence of the hazards associated with operating in the waters, especially at night. *Massachusetts*' antiaircraft guns fired on one of the mines, attempting to detonate it, but were unable to hit the target.

On July 19 the task group withdrew to a fueling rendezvous, with the refueling taking place on the twentieth. That same day, yet another main condenser leak brought about the need for the men of *Massachusetts* to lock shaft 3, at 0913. The repairs were completed by 1440, and the shaft was put back into service. Meanwhile, the antiaircraft battery practiced by firing at a drone.

Underway replenishment continued through July 22, with *Massachusetts* receiving fuel, provisions, and ammunition. The task group again made for southern Honshu on July 23, arriving at strike position in the early-morning hours of July 24, the targets being Japanese navy vessels in the Inland Sea. These strikes continued on July 25, targeting primarily ships in the Kure and Kobe areas. The task group withdrew for further replenishment on the twenty-sixth and twenty-seventh, resuming the assault on the Japanese ships in the Inland Sea on the twenty-eighth, before shifting to airfields and industrial targets near Tokyo on the twenty-ninth.

On the evening of July 29, Task Unit 34.8.1 (Bombardment Group Able) was formed, which included *Massachusetts*, *Indiana*, and flagship *South Dakota*, as well as cruisers *Quincy*, *Boston*, *St. Paul*, and *Chicago*. Also joining Able was Task Unit 37.1.8, which was HMS *King George V* and escorts.

The bombardment group steamed to Hamamatsu, where the target assigned to *Massachusetts* was the Japanese Musical Instrument Company, which, despite its innocent-sounding name, in fact at that time was that nation's second-largest producer of aircraft propellers, manufacturing both wooden and metal types.

Massachusetts' main battery opened fire at 2319 and ceased fire at 0028 on July 30, after having expended 270 rounds. In their November 18, 1945, assessment, the US Strategic Bombing Survey determined that eight rounds hit a recently acquired silk mill, destroying five mill buildings and seven bicycle sheds—the bicycles being critical to commuting workers.

The last day of July 1945 found *Massachusetts* retiring toward the fueling area, where she refueled the destroyer *Harrison* (DD-573) as she herself took on fuel from *Neosho*.

So confident were the men of *Massachusetts* that they were soon headed stateside that much of August 1 and 3 were spent transferring spare parts to sister ships *Indiana* and *South Dakota*, with *Brush* (DD-745) ferrying the parts between the ships as more units of the task group took on fuel. This process continued for several days, with *Massachusetts*' August 7 war diary noting, "In view of the impending departure of this ship for the mainland of the United States, various ships are placing personnel aboard for transportation, and we are receiving equipment and supplies as the ship is being cannibalized." Among the items transferred was Kingfisher 01481, which was transferred to *Indiana* to replace one of hers that had been lost in a crash.

At 1254 on August 9, *Massachusetts* and her escorts in Task Unit 34.8.1 began shelling the ironworks at Kamaishi, Honshu, making four passes at an average range of 14,000 yards. BB-59 by herself fired sixty-eight salvos totaling 265 high-capacity 16-inch rounds when ceasefire was signaled at 1445. Salvo 68 consisted of one round, the result of an ordnance casualty (hang fire) earlier on Salvo 60. This was caused by the failure of an operating-lever-latch plunger pin on the center gun of turret 2, which caused a burr in the plunger seat. The seat was deburred and a new plunger was installed. The gunnery officer of *Massachusetts*, Cmdr. Robert Odening, requested and received permission to clear the gun through the muzzle after the ceasefire signal. As a result, this round was fired twenty minutes after the other battleships had ceased fire, thus becoming the final 16-inch round fired against the enemy in World War II.

As *Massachusetts* was retiring from the bombardment area, a Judy was sighted to starboard, and the battleship's antiaircraft gunners opened fire with the enemy at a range of 11,000 yards and altitude of 14,000 feet and were soon joined by gunners aboard other ships, who together were able to drive off the aircraft.

Still off Honshu, on August 12, RAdm. Shafroth, commander of Battleship Squadron 2, shifted his flag from *South Dakota* to *Alabama*, the latter coming alongside *Massachusetts* to receive the flag silverware and china.

Since *Massachusetts* was now beyond her previously predicted day of departure for the United States, on August 14 the oiler *Aucilla* (AO-56) came alongside and took aboard the passengers who had previously come aboard *Massachusetts* for transportation stateside. The task force then steamed for a strike position off Tokyo.

At dawn on August 15, all the carriers in the task force launched aircraft for a strike against various targets in and around Tokyo. Shortly after the strike was launched, orders came down to cease all offensive operations against the Japanese. The strike was recalled, and the carriers defueled the aircraft and unloaded the ordnance upon the return of the strike aircraft; however, fighter combat air patrols continued to be maintained.

Massachusetts' war diary for August 16 notes she was "operating in area southeast of Tokyo, standing by while details of Japanese surrender are being arranged."

From August 19 to 21, "a 22[-]Boat Pool Party, a 12[-]man Ordnance Detail, the *Massachusetts* Marine Detachment, consisting of 4 officers and 91 men, Company "B" Bluejacket Landing Force and a Communication Team[,] were embarked in various ships and participated in the initial landings on the Island of Honshu, occupying the Naval Base at Yokosuka. All personnel returned aboard safely on 2 September 1945."

Company B of *Massachusetts* Bluejacket Landing Force consisted of four officers and 133 men, and the communication team of one officer and twenty-one men.

On August 23, Capt. Redman addressed the crew via the PA system, saying,

> Since the Japanese agreed to surrender on the 15th we have all witnessed a small part of the preparations for a very large

operation—the occupation of Japan. General MacArthur is the Allied Supreme Commander of the Occupation and Surrender. Admiral Nimitz is the United States' representative at the surrender and is, of course, in command of all naval forces involved. His flagship will probably be the *South Dakota*. The Third Fleet, under Admiral Halsey, has been greatly augmented by the addition of ships of all types, including transports and amphibious vessels, and reorganized so that in addition to Task Force 38, it now contains various forces for the landing occupation and support. Our own Marine and Bluejacket Companies are included. The job assigned to the rest of us is that of carrier support. Task Group 38.1 will cover the area of north Honshu and Hokkaido from a position off Kamaishi. The planes will maintain a Combat Air Patrol over the Jap fields to insure [*sic*] that any Japs who didn't get the word may be dealt with in the manner in which they have been accustomed. We will probably commence these flight operations on Saturday the 25th. On Sunday an advance airborne landing will take place at Atsugi Airdrome near Tokyo[,] and a force of battleships and other types will arrive in Sagami Wan, which is just outside Tokyo Bay itself, and some groups, such as minesweepers, will enter Tokyo Bay. On the 28th, airborne troops will land on Atsugi Airdrome[,] and naval and marine landing forces will occupy Yokosuka Naval Base in Tokyo Bay. Further landings will take place the following two days[,] and on 31 August the formal surrender will take place. Further landings including the large Army forces who will carry out the actual task of occupation [and] will follow as they are available. The necessity of keeping the maximum possible force ready for action until the surrender is actually accomplished and our forces are in control is obvious. After that the necessity of watching the Japs while they still have guns and planes remains, but it may be that, if all goes well, a few ships can be spared. We can only do the job we have and see what happens. We have no definite orders or information about overhaul, and I hesitate to risk another prediction. I will let you know when we do receive word.

That word came on August 28, as noted in the war diary: "During the afternoon a dispatch was received from ComThird Fleet indicating that this ship will leave for a period on the West Coast of the United States about September 3."

The diary noted on August 30 that "at the present time there are 6 officers and 370 enlisted men on board as passengers."

USS *Massachusetts* claimed the honor of having fired the first 16-inch shell in battle in World War II (at Casablanca in November 1942) and the last 16-inch shell of the war, at Kamaishi on August 9, 1945. This photo reportedly commemorates that last shot, from a 16-inch gun of turret 3. This ship in this photo has been mistakenly identified as USS *Indiana* when in fact it was *Massachusetts*, on the basis of a unique defect in the armor on the side of the turret, and the presence of the aforementioned curved frames on the front of the twin 5-inch/38-caliber gun mount in the background.

Upon the surrender of Japan, the US Navy furnished so-called Blue-Jacket Landing Forces to assist with the early stage of the Allied occupation of Japan. This Blue-Jacket Landing Force has assembled on the fantail of *Massachusetts* to prepare to go ashore to perform. The ship's war diary for August 1945 mentioned only one instance in which it dispatched a landing force: on the twentieth, in the Pacific some 300 nautical miles southeast of Tokyo. This force consisted of Company B, with four officers and 133 men; at about noon that day, the landing force was transferred to the high-speed transport USS *Gosselin* (APD-126) for transport to their assigned area at Yokosuka Naval Base, in the southwestern part of Tokyo Bay.

A supply of 16-inch shells have been brought to the main deck of *Massachusetts* alongside one of the turrets on September 12, 1945. The ship was homeward bound, one day out from Puget Sound, Washington. On the following day the ship would anchor at the US Navy's ammunition-storage facility at Sinclair Inlet, near the Puget Sound Navy Yard, and on September 14 the crew would unload the ammunition from the ship, for storage at the facility, in preparation for the ship's entering drydock at the navy yard.

Members of Company B, Blue-Jacket Landing Forces, are checking their equipment, including packs, ammunition boxes, and two .30-caliber machine guns on tripods, prior to being transferred to USS *Gosselin* for transport to Yokosuka Naval Base.

CHAPTER 5

Stateside!

On September 2, Task Group 30.3, including *Massachusetts*, formed up and refueled, prior to beginning to steam at 16 knots toward Puget Sound at 0800 the next morning. At 0107 on September 13, *Massachusetts* lookouts spotted Tatoosh Light on the coast of Washington, at the entrance to the Strait of Juan de Fuca. At 1947, *Massachusetts* anchored in the berth known as Charlie, Sinclair Inlet, Navy Yard, Puget Sound; her sailors had come home at last.

Two days later, the passengers debarked, along with the first leave party, consisting of twenty-three officers and 862 men, who were granted one-month leave.

On September 19, *Massachusetts* entered Dry Dock 4, with the war diary giving this overview of the work to be done: "Ship is to receive an extensive overhaul to include work on boilers, various parts of engineering plant; propellers, navigation bridge, flag plot, staff accommodations, etc., and installation of new radars, fire control gear and other equipment, moving of C.I.C. to below armor, etc."

This work was originally scheduled to be accomplished in sixty days but would be repeatedly extended, in large part due to the overwhelming workload faced by the navy yard, given the influx of returning ships.

On October 14, after the return of the men on leave, the second half of the ship's crew was granted a thirty-day leave. As of December 1, the completion date for the overhaul had been reset for December 26, and 950 enlisted personnel had been transferred for discharge. On December 8, *Massachusetts* left Dry Dock 4 and tied up at Pier 3 in the Navy Yard.

Massachusetts' war diary entry for December 18, 1945, noted,

Overhaul interrupted by the arrival of a large number of ships assigned to "Magic Carpet" operation requiring high[-]priority[-] voyage repairs. A very small amount of work is to continue on the overhaul, but the commandant of the Naval Base estimates that there will be at least a ten[-]day delay. USS Essex and Shangri-La similarly had their overhauls interrupted. Unofficial estimates indicate that the shipyard has more ships under overhaul than at any other time in its history.

Regarding *Massachusetts* in particular, the diary noted, "There remains about five to ten days['] work in the Navy Yard outstanding."

The diary entry for the final day of 1945 read,

When *Massachusetts* entered Dry Dock No. 4 at the Puget Sound Navy Yard, Bremerton, Washington, on September 19, 1945, a refitting of the ship began, which would last the rest of the year and prepare her for service in the postwar US Navy. This included work on the boilers and other components of the engineering plant, the propellers, the navigation bridge, and other areas. New radars and fire-control equipment would be installed, and the combat information center (CIC) would be relocated belowdecks. The ship is shown after her prolonged overhaul, on January 22, 1946. *US Navy via A. D. Baker III*

As seen in a head-on aerial view of *Massachusetts* undergoing postrefitting trials in Puget Sound on January 22, 1946, the quadruple 40 mm gun mounts had been removed from the foredeck and the roof of turret 2. The navigating bridge to the front of the conning tower had been enclosed with windows and a top. On the platform partway up the foremast was a new, round, SK-3 air-search radar antenna, above which may be seen a relatively small SG-1b surface-search radar antenna. *US Navy via A. D. Baker III*

U.S.S. MASSACHUSETTS (BB59)
DEAD AHEAD
PUGET SOUND, WN.
JAN. 22, 1946
SPEED- 6 KNOTS

Ship remains at anchor in Sinclair Inlet with status of overhaul completion still indefinite. Five to ten days['] shipyard work are still outstanding. Ship has made considerable progress on ammunition loading, personnel training[,] and general readiness for limited operations. The personnel situation is acute, but the period of "frantic" demobilization appears to have passed and it is now possible to plan more orderly training and turn-over of duties of men to be discharged. There are now 873 enlisted personnel aboard, 1147 having been transferred for discharge since arrival in the United States on 13 September. There has been a very large turnover of officer personnel, but the ship remains well over allowance, chiefly because of the large number of ensigns received. The ship[']s future employment is now relatively clear. Bureau of Personnel allowance of 23 officers and 407 enlisted will be effective on actually joining Third (Reserve) Fleet. USS *Massachusetts* is assigned as flagship of Commander of Third Fleet and as part of Battleship Division Three [with *Indiana* and *Alabama*]. Permanent mooring will apparently be provided in San Pedro or San Francisco area, and ship will remain in complete material readiness.

Overhaul at last complete, *Massachusetts* steamed for California on January 28, 1946. California newspapers reported in February 1946 that not only would *Massachusetts* be a part of the ready reserve fleet, with the familiar appellation Third Fleet, but that the commander of that fleet, VAdm. Howard F. Kingman, "is aboard the cruiser *Quincy*, temporary flagship here, pending arrival of the battleship *Massachusetts*." Indeed, on February 25, Kingman transferred his flag to *Massachusetts*.

However, on March 29, 1946, the US Navy announced its Postwar Plan Number 2. The plan directed the shift of *Massachusetts* and *South Dakota* from the Ready Reserve Fleet to the Inactive Atlantic Fleet, and *Alabama* and *Indiana* to the Inactive Pacific Fleet.

The plan also revealed the disposal of *Idaho* (BB-42) and *New Mexico* (BB-40), originally slated for the Sixteenth (Reserve) Fleet, as well as *Augusta* (CA-31), *Chester* (CA-27), *Louisville* (CA-28), *Portland* (CA-33), *Nashville* (CL-43), *Phoenix* (CL-46), *Boise* (CL-47), and *Saint Louis* (CL-49), all already serving with the Sixteenth Fleet. CruDiv 5, comprising *Baltimore* (CA-68), *Boston* (CA-69), *Canberra* (CA-70), and *Quincy* (CA-71), was to shift from the Third Fleet to the Nineteenth Fleet, and CruDiv 14, consisting of *Cleveland* (CL-55), *Columbia* (CL-56), *Montpelier*

A photo of the ship from astern confirms that the quadruple 40 mm gun mount and splinter shield, flanked by a 20 mm gun on each side, remained in place atop turret 3. On the turret roof to the front of the quadruple 40 mm gun mount was a redesigned tub for the director of that gun mount; it now had a curved, instead of flat, front. *US Navy via A. D. Baker III*

(CL-57), *Denver* (CL-58), and *Manchester* (CL-83), was to shift from the Fourth Fleet to the Sixteenth (Inactive) Fleet.

Massachusetts got underway from San Francisco Bay on April 4, 1946, bound for the East Coast. She anchored in Hampton Roads, Virginia, the morning of April 22, 1946, and at 0942 the crew manned the rails to render honors to President Truman, who was aboard the new carrier *Franklin D. Roosevelt*, as she passed by.

On May 20, *Massachusetts* entered Norfolk Naval Shipyard for inactivation. Processing the ship into the reserve fleet was a complex operation. One of the first steps was to dewater the ship. Water inlets for machinery as well as household uses (firefighting, sanitation, etc.) were sealed, water was drained from the miles of piping in *Massachusetts*, followed by the lines being blown by compressed air, and finally a rust preventative was fogged into the pipes. Then, various outside openings were sealed, including portholes, hatches, ventilators, funnels, and the openings around the 16-inch and 5-inch guns. Certain pieces of machinery, such as turbines, were opened and preservatives were applied. The ship was divided into zones, and each zone was equipped with dehumidification equipment. Spaces, such as fuel tanks, that could not reasonably be joined to a dehumidification zone had desiccant disks placed inside. The 20 mm and 40 mm antiaircraft barrels were removed from their mounts, and igloo-like domes were erected over the 40 mm mounts, with desiccant packs placed inside the domes prior to them being sealed.

Underwater, an impressed-current cathodic protection system was installed to minimize the electrolytic action of salt water. The waterline of any ship not in operation is especially vulnerable to corrosion, the result of alternate exposure to air and water as waves lap at the hull; as a result, an especially heavy coating of boot topping was applied.

On September 3, 1946, the status of *Massachusetts* was changed to "In Commission, In Reserve" during a brief ceremony at the Norfolk Naval Shipyard.

The next year, on March 27, she was decommissioned. For the first few years in the reserve fleet, she was tied up in Berth 1 at the Naval Shipyard in Portsmouth, but in late 1950 she was towed to Pier 8 at Newport News Shipbuilding and Dry Dock Company. Then, in 1951, she was shifted to Pier 12 across the Southern Branch at the Naval Annex in St. Helena.

However, *Massachusetts* and the other South Dakota–class battleships (as well as the other battleships in the reserve fleet) were not merely tucked away and forgotten. Rather, in addition to regular routine maintenance, the ship, at least during her early years in the reserve fleet, was given quinquennial drydocking for inspection and maintenance and had various modifications performed.

Massachusetts was steaming at 6 knots when this aerial photo was taken off her port beam on January 22, 1946. Noticeable alterations had been made to the upper part of the mainmast since the summer 1944 refitting, and an SR-a secondary air-search radar antenna was mounted on the platform near the top, and an SG-1b surface-search radar antenna was atop the small upper mast. *US Navy via A. D. Baker III*

Massachusetts wore the Measure 22 camouflage scheme shown here from October 1942 until January 1947. This scheme featured Navy Blue on the lower hull, up to the lowest point of sheer. Above that, the vertical surfaces were Haze Gray, and the decks were Deck Blue. In January 1947, she was repainted into the overall Haze Gray scheme known as Measure 13—the scheme she wears to this day. From her May 1942 commissioning until October 1942, she wore camouflage Measure 12, a mottled Navy Blue and Ocean Gray hull, as seen on page 23 of this book.

A final view of *Massachusetts* from January 22, 1946, shows the quadruple 40 mm gun mounts on the fantail, on the deck to the sides of the guns of turret 3, on the roof of turret 3, and on and adjacent to the aft part of the superstructure. Numerous 20 mm gun mounts also remained in place.

An April 2, 1952, list of outstanding alterations due to be performed included, in part, the following:

ShipAlt No:

592: Remove all 20 mm mounts in excess of 16–20 mm twins.

620: Replace watertight doors in gun blast area

633: Provide additional control of heavy machine gun battery

639: Remove BN Series radar associated with surface search radar equipment.

643: Install SG-6 radar on the foremast

699: Install Gun Sight Mk. 20 on 20 mm Twin Mounts Mk. 24.

715: Install ultimate 3"/50-caliber mounts.

731: Reduce number of onboard 36" searchlights to 1

Not all these alterations were performed, some being deferred. One very noticeable alteration that was performed was the removal of *Massachusetts'* aircraft catapults and associated gear. This was done about the time of the outbreak of the Korean War, as the US Navy planned to replace carrier-launched airplanes with helicopters. While Mamie lost her catapults, she was not equipped for the helicopters.

While Navy regulations as a rule forbade the removal of gear from ships in the reserve fleet, the result of painful lessons learned between the world wars, it is worthwhile to point out that during the Korean War, during which all four of the Iowa-class battleships were in operation, all four of those ships were home-ported in Norfolk. Thus, to this author, it seems likely that some of the gear removed from *Massachusetts* was removed during this period to support the Iowas.

In June 1959, only a few months after her superstructure was repainted, a below-waterline damage control valve failed and *Massachusetts* took on 66,675 gallons of water, causing a 3-degree list and her bow to settle about 8 inches. A Navy diver subsequently used a wooden plug to stop the leak.

Massachusetts remained laid up in Norfolk into the early 1960s. During her time in the reserve fleet, various concepts for modernization of the ship were considered. On June 27, 1961, Adm. Arleigh Burke, the chief of naval operations, designated the four South Dakota–class battleships as eligible for disposal, and *Massachusetts* was stricken from the Naval Register on June 1, 1962.

However, even before she was stricken, efforts were underway to preserve the ship. The first such effort was from the Portsmouth (Virginia) Chamber of Commerce. On January 7, 1962, the

This photo, taken from Telegraph Hill in San Francisco, shows *Massachusetts*, flanked by sister ships *Alabama* (*port*) and *Indiana* (*starboard*) in early 1946. For a brief period, *Massachusetts* was the flagship of Battleship Division 3, which consisted of these three veteran battlewagons, all of which were in reserve. *Naval History and Heritage Command*

Virginian-Pilot and Portsmouth Star reported that the organization had met with governor-elect Abertis Harrison concerning the ship, and that he had asked the Portsmouth legislators to meet with him while the general assembly was in session to determine the feasibility of establishing a state battleship commission. The newspaper also reported that Representative Porter Hardy Jr. was contacting the Navy to determine if the ship could be made available to the state.

The executive director of the chamber was quoted as saying that

> our interest in the ship is two-fold. First, since the Naval Shipyard is the first naval installation in the area and since the entire area is the largest naval concentration in the world, it is only fitting and proper that a major ship of the fleet be placed on permanent exhibit.
>
> Second, it will constitute a major tourist attraction which will draw literally thousands of people to Portsmouth. This has been proven in Texas[,] where last year 250,000 people visited the battleship *Texas*.

Garland pointed out that the *Massachusetts* is anchored only a few hundred yards off Portsmouth[,] and the cost involved

After the end of World War II, the US Navy was under orders to demobilize thousands of sailors, which left ships such as USS *Massachusetts* severely understaffed. Gradually, more personnel were inducted into the Navy, such as this small group of men who are being sworn into the service on the foredeck of USS *Massachusetts*, moored to Pier 33 in San Francisco, California, on or around March 19, 1946. In the background is one of her sister ships, very likely USS *Alabama*, since another photograph exists of these two ships docked together, in the order shown here, in San Francisco on March 17, 1946.

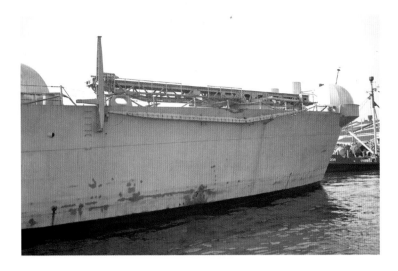

In March 1947, *Massachusetts* was decommissioned at the Norfolk Naval Shipyard, in Portsmouth, Virginia. She then was transferred to the Atlantic Reserve Fleet and was placed in long-term storage. The aft port area of the hull of *Massachusetts* is depicted in a photo dated January 26, 1948. Dome-shaped "igloos" had been placed over the splinter shields for the 40 mm gun mounts, to keep out the elements. Along the upper part of the hull is a boat boom in its stowed position. Boat booms could be swung out when the ship was at anchor, to provide a mooring point for the ship's boats. To the immediate front of the boom is the kingpost; cables would be rigged from the top of the kingpost to the outer end of the boat boom, to support the boom.

The battleship *Massachusetts* is in the right background, in long-term storage at the Norfolk Naval Shipyard in December 1949. The battleship is painted overall in a light-gray paint, likely Haze Gray. In the foreground is USS *Mississippi*. Originally a New Mexico–class battleship (BB-41) launched and commissioned in 1917, *Mississippi* was converted to a gunnery training ship (AG-128) soon after the end of World War II.

On June 1, 1962, the US Navy, anticipating no more need for the battleship *Massachusetts*, struck her from the Naval Vessel Register. Among the movable items rescued from the ship at that time was a hand-painted flag of the state of *Massachusetts*, which two sailors are exhibiting. *Naval History and Heritage Command*

Massachusetts is moored to a dock at Norfolk Naval Shipyard, Virginia, on January 3, 1963. At that time, she had been stricken from the Naval Vessel Register and was awaiting her fate. To the right is the attack cargo ship USS *Uvalde* (APA-88). *Naval History and Heritage Command*

The battleship is viewed from the aft starboard quarter while stored at the Norfolk Naval Shipyard, Virginia, on January 3, 1963. The catapults had been removed sometime after 1948. Several sheds had been positioned on the afterdeck and the top of turret 3, including one over the plenum chamber on the center of the deck aft of turret 3. *Naval History and Heritage Command*

In April 1963, YOS-14, an oil-storage barge normally assigned to the Craney Island Dredged Material Management Area, near Norfolk, was brought alongside *Massachusetts*, to serve for a receptacle for fuel oil that was to be pumped out of the spaces in the bottom of the hull. Defueling was a key step in preparing a retired ship for scrapping. *Naval History and Heritage Command*

In the early 1960s, when the US Navy was planning for the scrapping of *Massachusetts*, former crewmen formed an association to try to save the ship. Ultimately, the City of Fall River, Massachusetts, agreed to accept *Massachusetts* as a museum ship. Through donations from the public, the association raised enough money to have the battleship towed from Norfolk to Fall River. She is seen here being towed from the Norfolk Naval Shipyard at the beginning of her transit to Fall River in June 1965. *Naval History and Heritage Command*

Massachusetts is viewed head on as she departs, under tow, from the Norfolk Naval Shipyard. The "igloos" had been removed from the 40 mm gun mounts, and the fire-control radar antennas had been remounted on the secondary-battery directors (although all of them are out of alignment) and on the aft main-battery director, but not the forward one. Air- and surface-search radar antennas were not mounted. Flying from the yardarm was a Revolutionary War "pine tree" ensign of the state of Massachusetts Navy. *US Navy via A. D. Baker III*

Massachusetts is navigating Narragansett Bay, Rhode Island, under tow and with the assistance of a tugboat, during the final leg of her voyage from Norfolk to Fall River, on June 12, 1965. Later that day, the ship would arrive at her final destination, Fall River. *US Navy via A. D. Baker III*

Entering Fall River, Massachusetts, on June 12, 1965, *Massachusetts* passes under the not-yet-completed Charles M. Braga Jr. Memorial Bridge. The battleship's final berth would be just out of the view to the left of the photo, in what is now known as Battleship Cove.

in moving her would be negligible compared to the expense involved in towing the USS North Carolina from New Jersey to its home state.

Ultimately, the effort to keep the battleship near the shipyard failed. However, the proposed scrapping of the ship spurred not only her veterans' organization but also some Massachusetts politicians into action.

Representatives Torbert H. MacDonald and Thomas Lane contacted Massachusetts governor John Volpe in June 1962, suggesting that the state form a battleship commission to preserve the ship, and by the end of the month the Navy had agreed to temporarily postpone the sale of the ship for scrap. Ultimately, there would be at least seven such postponements. Governor Volpe was replaced by Governor Endicott Peabody in January 1963, and while Peabody was willing to ask the Navy to continue delaying the sale of the ship, he was unwilling to commit state funds or resources to move or preserve the vessel.

Thus, the *Massachusetts* veterans' association, joining with veterans' organizations in her namesake state, began a citizens' campaign to receive custody of the ship, forming the USS Massachusetts Associates. The Navy in turn sought assurances that the group could provide a suitable berth and the funding to move the ship, as well as ongoing funding for maintenance. On

February 10, 1964, the USS Massachusetts Memorial Committee was incorporated to raise the funds to achieve these goals.

The committee began an energetic campaign to raise the funds required, and on May 15, 1964, the Navy informed Congress of its intent to transfer custody of the ship, and that it was anticipated that Congress would approve this action on July 15.

The initial intent was to berth the ship in Boston. In fact, the *Berkshire Eagle* reported on July 9, 1964, that

the famed World War II battleship USS *Massachusetts*—"Big Mamie" is coming home to Boston next month as a permanent memorial to the state's war dead.

The ship's final voyage is scheduled so she will arrive in Boston Harbor Aug. 14, the 19th anniversary of VJ Day.

However, longshoremen in Boston were opposed to this, fearing that docking the 680-foot-long battlewagon at one of the city's piers would reduce the income potential for their union members. Thus, efforts began in earnest to find an alternate port for the battleship.

This led the committee to contact Fall River mayor Roland G. Desmarais, who embraced the idea immediately, despite the city having only one pier. He turned to the manager of that pier, Bill Torpey, to represent the city with the project. Within days, the Fall

River site had been agreed upon, but the movement of the ship was not nearly so prompt as the *Berkshire Eagle* had reported.

On May 9, 1965, a volunteer group of thirty-two Navy reservists from Massachusetts arrived in Norfolk to prepare the ship for towing. Finally, on June 8, 1965, the seagoing tug Margaret Moran began towing the battleship to Fall River. Aboard were twenty-six crew, including eleven veteran crewmen who had served aboard during World War II. With thousands of people looking on, she arrived in Narragansett Bay on June 12 and tied up in the Taunton River, parallel to, and in the shadow of, the then-incomplete Charles M. Braga Jr. Memorial Bridge. After contractors repainted the hull and superstructure, and a great deal of volunteer effort went into sprucing up the ship, the main deck of the ship was opened to the public by August. On August 14 the memorial was formally dedicated.

On June 10, 1968, *Massachusetts* was moved to her permanent mooring, perpendicular to the bridge. This would be the last movement of the ship until November 4, 1998, when she was moved to the South Boston Shipyard for repairs.

Back in 1987 it had been discovered that the battleship was badly in need of drydocking. Rust and electrolysis had reduced the thickness of the underwater hull plating by 50 percent in some places, some fuel tanks had been opened to the sea, and thousands of rivets were leaking. Although the Massachusetts legislature passed a six-million-dollar appropriation for hull work in 1988, trouble with the state budget caused this work to be postponed, repeatedly, until finally, in 1998, the work began.

During the drydocking, her outer, five-blade propellers were removed. The drydocking was complete on March 4, 1999, and the ship was towed back to Fall River and the memorial reopened.

Massachusetts rests at her new home in Battleship Cove in a 1966 photograph. Since then, the venerable battleship, which saw action from North Africa to the Pacific, has been preserved as a museum ship and a memorial to *Massachusetts'* war dead in World War II. In addition to well-preserved *Massachusetts*, Battleship Cove is home to several other historic ships and craft and the Maritime Museum. *Naval History and Heritage Command*

CHAPTER 6
Massachusetts Today

Since 1965, USS *Massachusetts* (BB-59) has made her home at Battleship Cove in Fall River, Massachusetts. The ship has been designated a national historic landmark and hosts large numbers of visitors year round.

The ship's number on the bow, 59, represents USS *Massachusetts'* designation, BB-59, signifying it was the fifty-ninth contracted battleship of the US Navy. It is white with a black shadow and is consistent with the post–World War II Measure 13 paint scheme.

As viewed from the forward end of the foredeck, USS *Massachusetts'* two forward 16-inch/45-caliber turrets are dominated by the superstructure and forward fire-control tower rising above them. The forward turret was designated turret 1, while the one immediately aft of it was turret 2. During a refit in mid-1944, two quadruple ("quad") 40 mm gun mounts were placed in raised tubs on the foredeck, midway between the photographer's vantage point and turret 1, but these were removed after the end of the war. Whereas *Massachusetts* had only six quad 40 mm gun mounts in mid-1942, by August 1944 her complement of these mounts had increased to eighteen.

In the foreground on the foredeck is the port anchor chain, with a short chain called a stopper, to the right, affixed to the anchor chain with a pelican hook and attached at the other end to the deck, to secure the chain in place and take the strain off the windlass.

Two single 20 mm Oerlikon gun mounts are on the foredeck of USS *Massachusetts*. Each one is partially protected by a curved splinter shield attached to the deck. The gunner received a degree of extra protection from the armored shield fastened to the mount. Visible are the tripod stand, armored shield, and details of the splinter shield, with its diagonal braces for this mount. Aft of the mount is the port hawsepipe; to the left is a watertight hatch.

The gunner manipulated the train (or traverse) and elevation of the 20 mm gun by strapping himself into shoulder rests on the gun carriage (not present here) and using his body to aim the piece. Atop the 20 mm gun's receiver are a drum-shaped sixty-round magazine and part of a ring sight. The gun had a theoretical rate of fire of 450 rounds per minute, so the loader kept busy removing empty magazines and installing full ones as fast as possible. Grab handles are on the front and rear of the magazine.

The starboard 20 mm gun mount currently on the foredeck lacks a shield and ammunition magazine. Instead of the ring sight, the Mk. 14 computing sight was often mounted on these guns, enabling gunners to better track fast-moving aircraft.

The starboard forward 20 mm gun and splinter shield are viewed from the center of the foredeck. Numerous 20 mm antiaircraft gun mounts were added or deleted throughout World War II, but the two forward mounts on the foredeck survived.

The two hawsepipes on the foredeck (the starboard one is shown), seen in several preceding photos, are where the anchor chains pass down through the bow. When raised, the shanks of the anchors are housed in the hawsepipes.

The aft portion of the starboard hawsepipe is viewed; the grille over the pipe is intended to prevent falling into the pipe. Two stoppers are fastened with pelican hooks to the anchor chain; the stoppers are attached to the white-painted pad eyes on the deck.

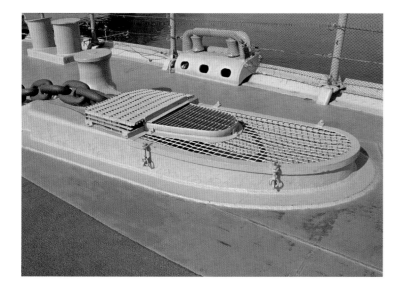

The port hawsepipe and the protective grilles over it are visible. Light-duty dogs hold down the forward section of grille. Along the deck in the background are several mooring chocks, a mooring bitt, and stanchions for the guard ropes and nets.

The port hawsepipe is seen facing aft. Four metal tabs welded to the rim of the grille serve to engage the dogs, which hold down the grille to the raised coaming of the hawsepipe. A single bitt is incorporated into the rear corner of the hawsepipe coaming.

A roller chock is provided on each side of the foredeck. Mooring lines, or hawsers, would pass through this chock. The rollers were intended to reduce chafing on the lines; a severed mooring line could result in dangerous or disastrous circumstances both for ship and crew.

The forward part of the foredeck was made from welded steel plates. In the foreground on the deck can be seen the faint contours of where an anchor washboard (a recessed platform for a spare anchor) once sat. This area subsequently was home for a 40 mm quad mount and ultimately was filled in and brought flush with the rest of the deck.

The anchor chains pass through riding chocks, or fairleads, partway between the hawsepipes and the windlasses. Attached to the deck below the anchor chains are chafing plates, to protect the deck from the grinding action of the anchor chains when in use.

Fastened to the deck between the riding chocks are four pad eyes, painted white, two of which are fitted with shackles. These pad eyes served to secure stoppers. Aft of the pad eyes is the bottom of a ship's anchor, on display here.

The display anchor is viewed facing forward on the foredeck, with the shackle at the top of the stock of the anchor in the foreground. At the other end of the anchor are the flukes. To the left in this photo, a good view is provided of a pelican hook on an anchor-chain stopper.

The port anchor chain passes through this riding chock, or fairlead. The view is facing aft. The rear of the visible part of the anchor chain is engaged around the port wildcats. Part of the windlass, the wildcat was a drum that raised and lowered the anchor.

Forward of the port wildcat is this raised watertight hatch. The door hinged to the top of the hatch coaming has a small, circular scuttle with a locking handwheel. To the front of the hatch is a red fire main. Aft of the hatch is a capstan for operating mooring lines.

To the left of the capstan is the port windlass. The drum of the windlass is called the wildcat and has indentations that engage the anchor chain links, acting similarly to a drive sprocket in raising or lowering the chain. To the far left is the starboard wildcat.

Aft of the wildcats is the breakwater, a low bulwark across the main deck intended to divert waves that crash on the deck from flowing into the area of the forward 16-inch gun turrets. The muzzles of those guns are fitted with tompions to seal off the barrels.

From each wildcat, the anchor chain is routed down the chain pipe to the chain locker. Aft of each of the wildcats are two handwheels on pedestals; one controlled the speed and direction of movement of the chain, and the other was for braking the chain.

The front facet of the breakwater slants forward at the top. The top of the breakwater is rolled, to afford protection to personnel who might bump into it. Abutting the center rear of the breakwater is a plenum chamber with four circular cover plates.

Stowed to each side of the plenum chamber aft of the breakwater is a paravane, a towed device designed to detonate mines or sever their anchoring cables. The paravane is viewed from the front, showing the wing mounted over the body.

Viewed from the starboard side, the breakwater is stiffened at the rear by triangular braces. On the near side of the paravane is a ventilator, and on the opposite side of the paravane is the plenum chamber. The front of the teak part of the deck is at the right.

The foredeck is viewed from behind the starboard side of the breakwater, showing the contrast between the teak deck in the foreground and the steel-plate deck forward of the breakwater. A small ladder with two treads is mounted on the plenum chamber.

To deploy the paravane, a boom would be erected on the side of the hull, and the paravane, tethered to the boom with a cable, would be lowered into the water. Thence, it would move away from the ship, gliding in water.

When deployed, a fin-type stabilizer was attached to the rear of the body of the paravane. Paravanes were effective in defeating moored mines and in detecting mined seaways, but they also decreased the speed, maneuverability, and endurance of the ship.

Looking across the front of the breakwater from the port side, the top of the port paravane is visible. Beyond the paravane is the top of the plenum chamber. To the far right is the front of turret 1, while to the left are the wildcats and windlass controls.

The front of turret 1 is viewed over the top of the port wildcat (*bottom*) and the plenum chamber. Black blast bags, or bloomers, are fitted over the barrels of the 16-inch/45-caliber guns to seal the gaps between the gun barrels and the fronts of the turrets.

The blast bags on the front of turret 1 are seen from the starboard side. Secured to the barrels with clamping bands, the blast bags were fabricated from rubberized fabric and were intentionally loose fitting, to accommodate the elevation and recoil of the guns.

The barrels of the three 16-inch/45-caliber Mk. 6 guns of turret 1 have three steps, or hoops. The "45-caliber" part of their designation indicates that the length of the barrel was forty-five times that of the bore of the gun; hence, the bore was 720 inches long.

The armored housing of the 16-inch turret was called the gunhouse. This is the starboard side of the gunhouse of turret 1, with turret 2 looming in the background. The armored face plates are 18 inches thick, while the side plates are 9.5 inches thick.

Projecting from the side of the gunhouse are hoods for the right trainer's (upper) and right pointer's (lower) telescopes. To the rear of the side of the gunhouse is the hood for the right side of the optical rangefinder; these hoods were nicknamed "ears."

The right rear side of turret 1 is viewed facing forward. The rear of the right rangefinder hood is to the right. Below the hood is a ventilator plenum on the side of the gunhouse. A larger ventilator plenum is prominent on the rear plate of the gunhouse.

The rear of the gunhouse of turret 1 is viewed from a different angle, showing the two ventilator plenums, fabricated from welded steel. The rear plate of the gunhouse is 12 inches thick. Faintly visible below the turret is a raised watertight hatch.

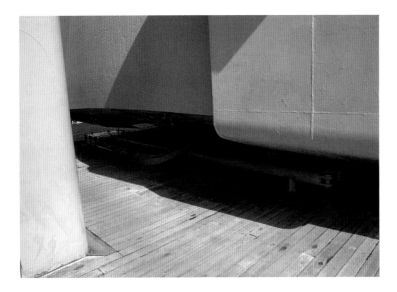

Stowed below the rear overhang of turret 1 are several tubular struts and a small davit, probably for lowering ammunition or cargo belowdecks. The hatch providing the crew with access into the gunhouse is located toward the center of the bottom of the overhang.

The front of the left hood for turret 1's rangefinder is viewed. The rangefinder's objective was protected by a sliding armored shutter, operated from within the gunhouse. The rangefinder operator's station was near the center rear of the gunhouse.

Visible on the port side of turret 1 are the left trainer's and pointer's telescope hoods and the left rangefinder hood. The ring-shaped base the gunhouse rests on is the top of the barbette, a heavily armored structure extending deep into the hull.

As observed from the navigating bridge of USS *Massachusetts*, the 16-inch/45-caliber guns of turrets 1 and 2 mutely stand watch over the Taunton River. The roof plates of the 16-inch gunhouses were fabricated from 7.25-inch armor plate. Multiple lateral tiers of oval-head slotted screws are visible; these secured the plates to the frame of the gunhouse. Toe rails are fitted around the forward and side edges of the roof. Two periscope heads are present on the roof of turret 1, visible on either side of the center gun of turret 2.

Jutting from the front of the barbette of turret 2 on the main deck level is a structure designated the deck office, and further designated as compartment A-101L. On the side of that structure adjacent to the barbette is a door with a handwheel lock.

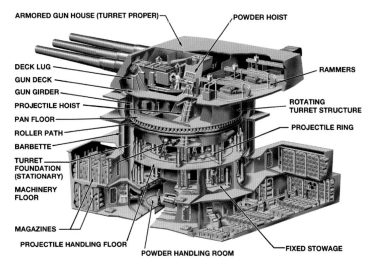

A diagram from a World War II US Navy gunnery manual illustrates how a 16-inch/45-caliber turret was much more than just the gunhouse and guns that were visible above the main deck. Extending far below were various levels for ammunition handling and for vital machinery.

Two quad 40 mm antiaircraft guns and guntubs were installed on the main deck to each side of turret 2 after USS *Massachusetts* was commissioned. Shown here is the starboard one. Rising above the guntub is the left side of the gun shield.

The quad 40 mm gun mount shown (*at left*) is viewed more closely. The cutouts at the bottom of the guntub let crewmen kick spent shell casings out of the tub, preventing fouling the mount. The cutouts also allowed water that washed into the tub to escape.

The starboard forward 40 mm gun mount is viewed from aft. The 40 mm mounts in this part of the main deck were not installed until 1944; prior to that, there was a gallery of 20 mm guns behind splinter shields in this area on each side of the main deck.

The same 40 mm gun mount shown in the preceding photos is seen facing forward. In addition to the cutouts in the front plate of the shield for the gun barrels, there are cutouts toward the sides for the pointer's and trainer's sights.

The starboard forward quad 40 mm gun mount is viewed from the rear. Seats are provided for the pointer, left, who manually elevated the guns, and the trainer, right, who traversed the mount. The platforms were for the loaders and the gun captain.

In a view of the lower front of the quad 40 mm gun mount, to the left are the seat and footrests for the trainer. In the foreground is the train power drive. The curved object at the center is a case discharge chute; three more of these chutes originally were present.

Aft of the forward starboard 40 mm gun mount is this angled facet of the first level of the superstructure. The door provides access to a corridor leading to several wardroom staterooms. Aft of the bottom of the ladder is a red-colored fire main.

This photo taken on the starboard side of the main deck around frame 80 shows how, aft of the angled facet of the superstructure, the first level of the superstructure runs parallel to the edge of the main deck. The door in the foreground leads to the flag office.

The section of main deck shown in the preceding photo appears at the bottom of this view of the starboard side of the superstructure. The South Dakota–class battleships were designed and constructed under tight size and weight constraints, which included a fairly compact arrangement of a single smokestack (*left*) abutting the rear of the forward fire-control tower (*upper center*), as seen here. Also, the secondary battery of twin 5-inch/38-caliber gun mounts was compactly arranged, with five mounts on each side of the superstructure. Four of the starboard 5-inch mounts, omitting the aft mount, are in this view. To the far right is the navigating bridge, above which is the top of the conning tower.

The starboard 5-inch/38-caliber gun mounts are visible here. The 5-inch mounts were assigned numbers, 1 through 10, forward to aft, with the odd numbers being on the starboard side and even numbers on the port side. Hence, from right to left, mounts 1, 3, 5, 7, and 9 are present in this photo. There are four Mk. 37 directors on the ship. These controlled the fire of the secondary battery of 5-inch/38-caliber guns. Two of the Mk. 37 directors are visible here, to the upper right and at the upper center. Each of these directors is topped with a Mk. 12 radar antenna with a Mk. 22 "orange peel" altitude-finding radar antenna next to it on the right side. To the far left is part of the boat crane.

This feature, also visible at the lower left in the preceding photo, is a Mk. 51 director (or Mk. 51 fire-control system, abbreviated FCS) protected by a splinter shield. Each Mk. 51 director controlled the operation of a quad 40 mm antiaircraft mount; in this case, the associated 40 mm mount is to the far left. This director is on the main deck at the same level as its associated 40 mm gun mount. More often, Mk. 51 directors were situated above and slightly away from their associated gun mounts, in order to give the director operator a better vantage point. Above this director is a stair landing, and above the landing, mounted on the superstructure, a ship's bell is partially visible.

The same Mk. 51 director seen in the preceding view is observed from aft. The part of the director visible above the top of the splinter shield is the front of a Mk. 15 lead-computing gunsight. The operator of the director manipulated the gunsight to track attacking aircraft, and the director computed the amount of lead necessary and electronically transmitted the firing solution to the associated quad 40 mm gun mount. If necessary, however, the gun crew could aim and fire the guns. The splinter shield has rolled top and side edges. Above the director is the right side of the shield (as the enclosure of the gun mount is called) of a twin 5-inch/38-caliber gun mount.

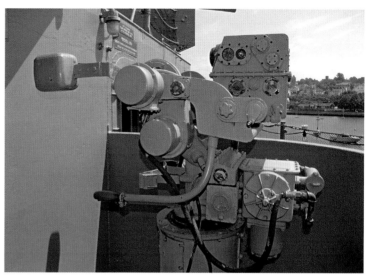

The right side of the same Mk. 51 director is in view. The right handlebar control curves down from the sight bracket. The mechanism with the round, spoked cover to the front of the director is an air pump, to supply compressed air for driving the gyro.

The Mk. 51 director, viewed from the rear, comprises a Mk. 15 gunsight mounted in a yoke on top of a pedestal attached to the deck. The unit included a gyro, which, when caged, was aligned with the gunsight's line of sight. When the operator acquired a target, began tracking it, and uncaged the gyro, the sight transmitted information to a computer, which calculated the necessary lead for the 40 mm guns. To track the target, the operator manipulated the bicycle-type handlebars. The two objects protruding to each side of the gunsight are counterweights. Before the Mk. 15 gun sight was introduced, the Mk. 14 gunsight was used in the Mk. 51 director. An auxiliary telescope also could be mounted on the sight.

Visible on the left side of a Mk. 51 director are the left handlebar control and the sides of the Mk. 15 gunsight and the air pump. Extending to the rear from the upper part of the director is the left counterweight. To the far left is the shield of a 40 mm gun mount.

The upper part of the Mk. 51 director, including the Mk. 15 lead-computing gunsight, is viewed from the front. This sight was a complex instrument, containing sophisticated optical and gyroscopic mechanisms. On the top half of the sight is the sight window.

The Mk. 15 director is observed from above. The operator stood between the two counterweights. The eyepiece is the dark fixture on the right rear of the sight. On top of the sight are two ring clamps for attaching an auxiliary telescope.

The 40 mm gun mount and guntub adjacent to the starboard aft corner of the superstructure are observed from above. Steps are present on the rear of the loaders' platform, and the guardrail at the rear of the mount was for the safety of the loaders. The four curved, vertical objects on the rear of the mount are spent-casing chutes.

The inner sides of the tubs for the quad 40 mm guns on USS *Massachusetts*, as well as other US navy ships in World War II, were covered with racks for stowing ready clips of 40 mm ammunition. These racks were removed from the guntubs after the war. The splinter shield was manufactured from fairly thin steel.

The quad 40 mm gun mount viewed in the preceding series of photos is observed from its aft quarter. Above the guns are a ship's bell and 5-inch gun mounts numbers 7 and 9. To the left is the aft section of the starboard side of the superstructure. Within this part of the superstructure on the main-deck level was crew's berthing. During the course of World War II, in the left foreground there were several different configurations of 20 mm antiaircraft cannons behind a splinter shield, but these were subsequently removed. To the upper left is the left rangefinder housing on turret 3. At the top, both the forward (*right*) and aft (*left*) Mk. 38 primary-battery directors are visible. These directors, nicknamed, respectively, Spot 1 and Spot 2, controlled the 16-inch/45-caliber guns.

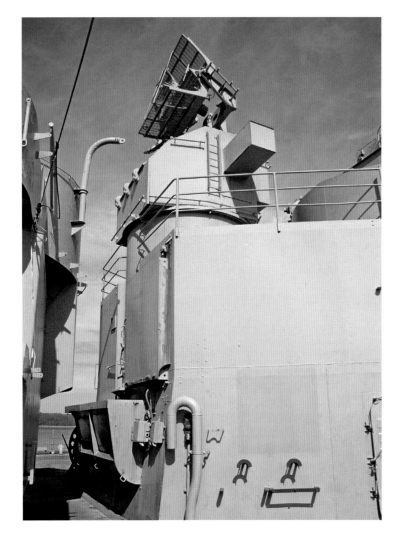

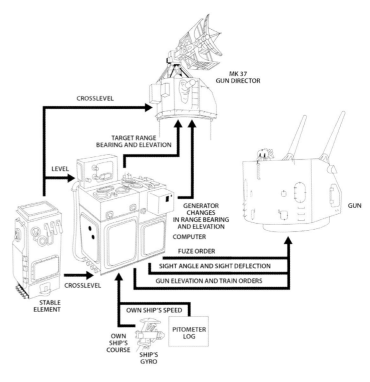

CROSSLEVEL

MK 37
GUN DIRECTOR

TARGET RANGE
BEARING AND ELEVATION

LEVEL

GENERATOR
CHANGES
IN RANGE BEARING
AND ELEVATION

COMPUTER

FUZE ORDER

SIGHT ANGLE AND SIGHT DEFLECTION

GUN ELEVATION AND TRAIN ORDERS

CROSSLEVEL

GUN

STABLE
ELEMENT

OWN SHIP'S SPEED

OWN
SHIP'S
COURSE

PITOMETER
LOG

SHIP'S
GYRO

Poised on a cylindrical base atop the rear point of the superstructure of USS *Massachusetts* is the aft Mk. 37 director. Inside the four Mk. 37 directors on the ship, operators—visually and with radar—spotted and tracked aerial or surface targets and communicated that information to a plotting room belowdecks, where that information was processed into firing solutions for the 5-inch guns. These directors could also control the 40 mm antiaircraft guns and, in emergencies, the 16-inch main battery. The director's armored housing enclosed an optical rangefinder and spotting telescopes, and mounted on top were radar antennas: in this case, a Mk. 12 antenna with a Mk. 22 "orange peel" antenna to the side.

The Mk. 37 secondary-battery director usually was tasked with tracking enemy aircraft and ships, primarily destroyers, and establishing their range, bearing, and, in the case of aircraft, altitude. Those data were transmitted to the plotting room ("Plot"), where analog computers, working with stable elements, which corrected for the pitch and roll of the ship, and the ship's gyro and pitometer, which provided information on the ship's course and speed, calculated within seconds the firing solution for the 5-inch guns. Plot sent that data to the director as well as the 5-inch turret and also controlled the train (traverse) and elevation of both the guns and the director. However, the director also made corrections to the target bearing, range, and angle of attack. Also, although the directors normally controlled the aiming and firing of the 5-inch guns, Plot or the gun crews could control the guns when necessary. Plot would control the guns when firing at targets ashore.

This view of the aft part of turret 3 from the starboard side provides a sense of the clearance between the rear of the gunhouse and the superstructure. Originally, a gallery of three 20 mm antiaircraft guns were positioned within a splinter shield on the roof of turret 3, but during a refitting during World War II, the quad 40 mm mount and guntub were installed atop the turret, and a 20 mm gun was mounted on each side of the 40 mm mount within a lower, semicircular splinter shield, seen here next to the 40 mm guntub. The 20 mm guns are no longer present within those splinter shields. Below the splinter shield for the 20 mm gun is the left rangefinder hood.

With the left front corner of turret 3 in the foreground, the 40 mm guntub atop the turret appears to the far right. At the center is the tub for the Mk. 51 director associated with the 40 mm gun mount directly behind it. The sight is missing from the director.

A closer view is provided of the quad 40 mm gun mount and guntub atop turret 3, showing the ladder rungs on the front of the tub and the handrail around the top of it. Details of the Mk. 37 director and its radar antenna array are also visible.

The 40 mm guns in the mount on turret 3 are visible above the splinter shield. Many of their parts and components have been stripped, including the spent-casing deflectors at the rears of the guns, but the automatic loader chutes atop the guns are still present.

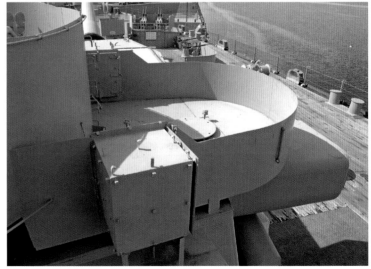

The right 20 mm gun station atop turret 3 is shown. The round mounting plate for the 20 mm gun is at the center of the position. In the foreground is an ammunition locker; on the forward side of the splinter shield is another ammunition locker. Extending below the gun station is the right rangefinder hood.

On each side of the main deck abeam turret 3 is a warping winch, used along with hawsers in docking the ship. Each winch has two drums, one on each side of the gearbox, for hauling on the hawsers. The winch motor is forward of the gearbox.

The starboard warping winch is viewed facing toward the stern of the ship. Directly aft of the winch are a splinter shield that originally enclosed several 20 mm antiaircraft guns. Just aft of that shield is a quad 40 mm mount that was a retrofit during World War II.

On the starboard side of the main deck just aft of the splinter shield shown in the preceding photo is a quad 40 mm gun mount in a guntub. The sloping top of the guntub allowed the guns to depress to fire on enemy planes approaching low off the beam.

In a view from the centerline of the main deck, facing forward, turret 3 and the superstructure loom in the background. Several hatchways leading belowdecks are in view. The low structure with the ladder up the side is a large ventilator plenum.

Turret 3, with its 16-inch/45-caliber guns elevated to different angles, is viewed from the after part of the main deck. Like the gunhouses of the other 16-inch main-battery turrets, the armor on turret 3's gunhouse is 18 inches thick on the front, 9.5 inches thick on the sides, 12 inches thick on the rear plate, and 7.25 inches thick on the roof. As built, there was a ladder on each side of the 16-inch guns on the front plate of each turret, but these ladders were removed at some point after January 1946. Each of these guns could sustain a rate of fire of about two rounds per minute, with a maximum range of approximately 37,000 yards, or 21 miles. During one of the rare instances where a US battleship exchanged fire with an enemy battleship during World War II, *Massachusetts* registered five 16-inch hits on the Vichy French battleship *Jean Bart* at Casablanca in November 1942, causing significant damage.

The aft port section of the superstructure of USS *Massachusetts* is viewed from the main deck to the side of turret 3. To the left are twin 5-inch/38-caliber gun mounts numbers 8 and 10. Forward of the Mk. 38 director is the mainmast, which replaced the smaller original mainmast during a 1945–46 refit. An SR-A secondary air-search radar antenna is installed near the top of the mainmast. Farther forward is the foremast, which carries an SK-3 air-search radar antenna. To the front of the mainmast is the forward fire-control tower, atop which is the forward Mk. 38 primary-battery director. To the left of that tower is the center port Mk. 37 secondary-battery director, with its suite of Mk. 12 and Mk. 22 radar antennas visible on top.

Lying along the port edge of the main deck abeam turret 3 are two kingposts for boat booms. When the kingposts were erected on the hull, cables running from their tops supported the boat booms, to which boats were moored when the ship was at anchor.

The port warping winch on the main deck abaft turret 3 is viewed facing forward. Along the edge of the deck in the background are the davit and the two kingposts for boat booms seen in the two preceding photos. To the right is the side of turret 3.

The port warping winch is viewed from the side, showing the spoked design of the drum. Two small lifting eyes are mounted on top of the gearbox, and one lifting eye is visible atop the motor.

The port side of the main deck aft of the superstructure is viewed from above, showing a hatchway and a ventilator in the foreground, the port warping winch in the middle distance, and the 20 mm gun gallery and the 40 mm gun tub in the background.

These 20 mm antiaircraft guns are on pedestal mounts behind a splinter shield on the port side of the main deck, aft of turret 3. The shields, comprising two armor plates that originally were fitted on the gun mounts, are no longer present. The handwheels on the pedestals were for raising or lowering the gun cradles, thus placing the guns at an optimal height for the gunner as he maneuvered himself to elevate or depress the piece. Above the guns are the brackets and eyepieces of the ring sights.

Aft of the 20 mm guns on the port side of the main deck are this quad 40 mm gun mount and tub, with an interpretative placard on the tub. To the right is the Mk. 51 director associated with this 40 mm gun mount, situated in a tub atop a pedestal.

The Mk. 51 director associated with the quad 40 mm gun mount in the preceding photo is viewed in relationship with the 40 mm gun mount it controlled. The director lacks a sight. The white object on the side of the tub is a recognition chart for Japanese aircraft. Fire hoses are stowed on the pedestal of the director. The pedestal that the director and tub are mounted on gave the operator of the director a better field of view over the adjacent quad 40 mm gun mount.

In a view from the rear of the superstructure, the port Mk. 51 director (*left*) and quad 40 mm gun mount (*right*) featured in the preceding photos are observed from above. In the background is the port fantail quad 40 mm gun mount and guntub.

The fantail, the aft part of the main deck, is clad with steel plate. Flanking the aircraft-handling crane at the center are two quad 40 mm gun mounts placed in guntubs, and two Mk. 51 director tubs positioned on pedestals. Two mooring bitts are to the right.

The fantail is observed from the port side. During World War II, the port aircraft catapult would have occupied much of the space in the right side of the photo. The two catapults and their foundations were removed while the ship was in mothballs after the war.

Although the two aircraft catapults are missing from USS *Massachusetts*, the aircraft-handling crane is still in place. It is observed from the starboard side of the stern. Flanking the crane are the two aft 40 mm gun mounts and their guntubs.

The lower part of the aircraft-handling crane is observed facing aft. The heel, or bottom of the crane boom, is mounted with pins to a base, which in turn rotates with the boom on the stand attached to the deck. Below the crane on the second deck is the crane's turning gear, while on the third deck is the hoisting gear. The placard is not original equipment.

To the aft starboard side of the aircraft crane are controls for the crane. From left to right, they are the hoisting-gear operating handwheel, emergency-brake hand lever, speed indicator and electrical control, and turning-gear operating handwheel.

The lower part of the aircraft-handling crane is viewed from its right side. Straddling the sheave at the center is the A-frame. Attached to the top of the A-frame is a tie-rod, the bottom of which is pinned to the arm extending to the rear of the base of the crane.

The boom of the crane is seen from its right side. Several spoked sheaves are visible on the crane, as well as two spotlights. When conditions necessitated it, such as in a severe storm, it was possible to lower the crane boom so that it lay flat on the deck.

The base of the crane and the stand below it are observed from the left side, showing the points where the boom (*left*) and A-frame (*right*) are pinned to the base. To the upper right is the lower part of the tie-rod that connects to the top of the A-frame.

The two tubs for the Mk. 51 directors associated with the two quad 40 mm gun mounts on the fantail are viewed facing forward. Oddly, the starboard tub has its rounded side and access ladder facing aft, while the port tub has its rounded side facing forward.

The aircraft-handling crane is viewed from the front, with a Mk. 51 director tub located to each side and a mooring chain running across the deck at the bottom of the photograph. The crane was designed to rotate at a rate of one-half revolution per minute when bearing a full working load. Faintly visible running up the rear of the crane is a ladder, to give riggers access to the upper part of the boom. A removable brace attached to the front of the crane helps stabilize the crane. At least one photo of USS *Massachusetts* during her time in commission shows such a brace installed.

The proximity of the port fantail Mk. 51 director tub to the guntub of the port quad 40 mm gun mount is illustrated. Both fantail director tubs currently have had the actual directors replaced by electrical equipment lockers, visible above the tops of the tubs.

The 40 mm gun mount and guntub on the port side of the fantail are similar in layout to those on the starboard side of the fantail. The informational placard is attached to the guntub, and the "Do not climb" stenciling on the gun barrel jackets was not present during wartime.

At the stern of USS *Massachusetts* is the flagstaff, from which the national ensign was flown when the ship was at anchor or docked between the hours of 0800 and sunset. The national colors were to be transferred from the gaff to the flagstaff at the moment the anchor was dropped. The flagstaff is set at a rearward angle so that it hangs over the stern. The disc-shaped object at the top of the flagstaff is the truck.

At the stern, a mooring chain passes through a chock equipped with a hinged retainer plate on top. Adjacent to the chock is the guntub of the port fantail quad 40 mm gun mount. The opening at the bottom of the guntub allows water to flow out.

USS *Massachusetts* is viewed from a distance at her berth in Battleship Cove, Fall River, Massachusetts. Visible here is a very pronounced feature of South Dakota–class battleships: a recess in the side of the hull just below the main deck, extending from forward of turret 2 to the rear of the superstructure. The purpose of the recess was to form a sort of shelf along the top of the ship's side tankage (i.e., at the bottom of the recess), to provide locations for the fuel-oil filler plates at the tops of the tanks. The tanks built into the side of the hull included air voids and fuel tanks. In addition to providing storage space for fuel, this system of voids and tanks provided antitorpedo protection to the most-vital internal spaces of the hull.

The method of attaching the blast bags, or bloomers, to the 16-inch guns is illustrated in this view of the front left corner of turret 1. A band-type clamp secures the bag to the gun, and the rear of the bag is attached to an angle-iron bracket surrounding the gunport. The rubber-impregnated canvas bloomers do not have an indefinite life span and are subject to deterioration from sunlight and the elements. Fortunately for *Massachusetts* and other preserved battleships, the US Navy's reactivation of the Iowa-class battleships during the Reagan administration and their subsequent deactivation in 1990–91 created fresh surplus supplies of these components.

This is the quad 40 mm gun mount and guntub on the main deck adjacent to the forward port corner of the superstructure. Conical flash suppressors are on the muzzle of each gun. The panels of the gun's shield are attached to the inner frame of the shield with slotted screws.

NUMBER OF LIGHT ANTIAIRCRAFT ARMAMENT MOUNTS ABOARD USS MASSACHUSETTS

Date	40 mm Quad	20 mm Single	20 mm Twin
May 1942	6	12	–
Nov. 1942	6	35	–
Jan. 1943	10	50	–
Feb. 1943	12	61	–
June 1944	16	52	1
Aug. 1944	18	32	1
Aug. 1945	15	22	8

Note: An experimental 20 mm quad mount was aboard from June 1944 through October 1945.

The quad 40 mm gun mount on the main deck adjacent to the forward port corner of the superstructure is seen from aft. The curved sections of teak planking on the deck in the foreground indicate the location of a splinter shield for a 20 mm gun that was removed.

From about frames 69 to 99, the first level of the superstructure runs parallel to the edge of the main deck, leaving a narrow walkway along that deck. This view illustrates a portion of the port side of that part of the superstructure, showing several of the doors and portholes. A semicircular rain deflector is mounted above the porthole in the foreground. The doors open outward, making for more constriction on the walkway when they were opened. Within view on the superstructure deck above are several of the 5-inch/38-caliber gun mounts.

Alongside the port aft end of the superstructure on the main deck is a quad 40 mm gun positioned inside a tub, corresponding to a similar gun mount on the opposite side of the main deck. This gun mount lacks the guardrails, the left gun's spent-casing deflector is missing, and the spent-casing chutes are no longer present. However, other key components are intact, including the ring sights and their brackets as well as the automatic loader assemblies on top of the receivers of the guns. In the left background is turret 3.

The starboard side of USS *Massachusetts* is observed. To the right is the ship's mooring quay. The features of the ship aft of the 40 mm guntub atop turret 3 are hidden by several other ships and boats on display at Battleship Cove, including the fleet submarine USS *Lionfish* (SS-298). The recess along the top of the hull is quite noticeable. Atop the foremast, located aft of the forward fire-control tower atop the superstructure, is a dish-shaped SK-3 air-search radar antenna. Aft of the foremast is the ship's sole smokestack. The single smokestack was a design consideration that grew out of the necessity to make the ship's above-decks structures as compact as possible, due to weight and size concerns.

The 16-inch/45-caliber guns of turret 2 are viewed from the starboard side of the main deck. Details of the right rangefinder hood of turret 1 are visible to the right. On the outboard side of the hood is an access plate, attached with hex screws to the hood.

The blast bags and front plate of turret 2 are observed up close. The armor of the frontal plates of the turrets was the thickest on the ship, at 18 inches. Not far behind was the armor of the conning tower, which was 16 inches thick on the sides.

On the right side of turret 2 is a re-creation of a cartoon painted on the turret during World War II, showing "George the Gremlin" riding a 16-inch projectile with Japanese and German flags painted on it. At the top left are the bridge and top of the conning tower.

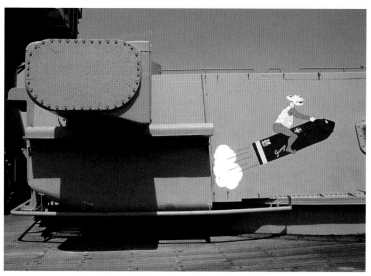

More of the right side of turret 2 is observed from the superstructure deck. Below the rangefinder hood is a ventilator plenum. Another ventilator plenum is on the rear of the turret; the top of the ventilator projects out from the trunk of the ventilator.

A view of the side of turret 2 taken from alongside the rear overhang shows toward the front the hoods for the right pointer's and trainer's telescopes. The pipe attached by brackets to the bottom of the gunhouse is a footrail that was retrofitted at some point.

The hatch to the gunhouse of turret 2 is in the bottom of the overhang. The platform under the hatch as well as the footrails enabled personnel to safely exit the turret when it was trained to the side; otherwise, it was a 10-foot fall to the main deck.

In a view facing forward from the front starboard side of the superstructure deck, turret 2 is to the left, a 40 mm gun mount is at the center, turret 1 is in the middle distance, and the foredeck is in the far distance. The stack next to turret 2 is not original equipment.

In a view of the starboard side of the superstructure deck, facing aft, the right rangefinder hood of turret 2 is to the right, above which part of the bridge is visible. Between the quad 40 mm gun mount and the 5-inch/38-caliber gun mount is a Mk. 51 director.

The forward part of the superstructure of USS *Massachusetts* is observed from the starboard side of the main deck, with part of turret 2 to the right and the bridge immediately above and aft of the turret. Rising above the rear of the bridge is the top of the conning tower, the heavily armored nerve center of the ship during battle. Just aft of the conning tower is the forward fire-control tower, complete with a yardarm and topped with the forward Mk. 37 secondary-battery director, while above and aft of that director is the forward Mk. 38 primary-battery director, "Spot 1."

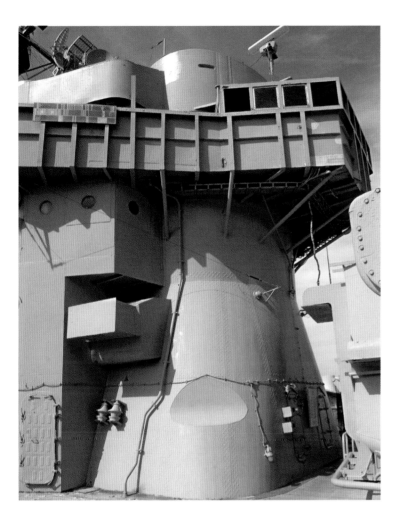

The board on the rear part of the bridge is painted with campaign ribbons representing the campaigns in which USS *Massachusetts* saw action.

As viewed from the starboard side, the conning tower has a pronounced taper from the level of the superstructure deck up to the level below the navigating bridge deck. Viewed from above, the upper part of the conning tower has an oblong shape, wider from side to side than from front to back. The navigating bridge was remodeled several times during and once after World War II. A 1946 refitting included the enlarging of the bridge, the installation of support struts underneath the bridge, and the addition of the enclosure at the center part of the bridge.

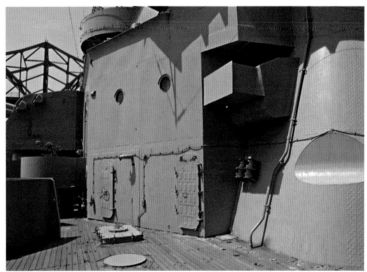

At the superstructure-deck level, the angled facet on the forward starboard side of the superstructure aft of the conning tower (visible to the right) has two doors on the first level, along with exposed electrical cables. The upper level has two portholes.

Adjacent to the angled facet of the port side of the superstructure on the superstructure deck is a quad 40 mm gun and guntub. The Mk. 51 director that controlled this gun mount is partly visible between the 40 mm guntub and the nearest 5-inch gun mount.

The Mk. 51 director on the superstructure deck, adjacent to the forward port facet of the superstructure, is viewed. The gunsight is not installed on the director, but the cradle and the two counterweights are visible. A spoked cover is present on one of the portholes.

The 5-inch/38-caliber mount number 1, on the starboard side of USS *Massachusetts*, is observed from below. The shield of the mount was formed of 2-inch-thick steel armor. The shields are about 15 feet wide, 10 feet high, and 16 feet from front to rear.

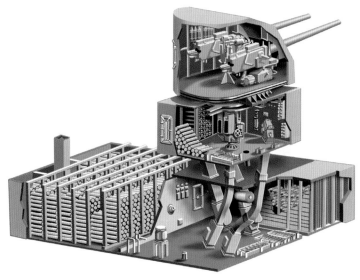

Directly beneath each of the dual-purpose 5-inch/38-caliber mounts was a ready service room, connected to the mount via hoists, which transported the shells and powder canisters. Farther below was the magazine and ammunition-handling room. From there the separately stowed powder and shells were fed to the ready service room via ammunition hoists.

As viewed from the right side of 5-inch/38-caliber gun mount 1, the protective hood for the trainer's sight protrudes above the access door. On the rear of the shield is an oblong crew access door with three rungs mounted on the armor below the door.

On the left side of the 5-inch/38-caliber shield are two armored hoods for sights. The forward hood is for the trainer's sight, while the hood behind it is for the sight checker, who ensured that the sights of the gun mount were laid on the designated target.

This space is on the superstructure deck between the superstructure (*right*) and 5-inch gun mount 3. The assembly that is shaped like a quarter of a cylinder, on the side of the superstructure, is a ventilator hood.

Resting on top of a raised structure that serves as the gun mount's upper ammunition-handling room is 5-inch gun mount 5. The view is facing aft. To the top left is the roof-hatch operating mechanism on the rear of the shield of 5-inch gun mount 3.

The rear of the shield of 5-inch gun mount 3 is displayed. The small door with the rounded bottom toward the bottom of the shield is for the case-ejection chute port. The small square door above it is for the auxiliary case-ejection port.

Gun mount 5 is viewed from farther back, showing the typical sight hoods for the trainer and the sight checker. An access door is on the side of the shield below the trainer's sight hood. Below the shield of the turret is the ring-shaped stand that the gun mount is mounted on. An oblong door leads into the upper ammunition-handling room below the gun mount. Over that door is a rain gutter in the shape of an inverted V. Four ladder rungs are on the side of the shield toward the top; other rungs below them have been removed, but the mounting holes for the screws that held the rungs in place are still apparent.

On the starboard side of the superstructure deck among the 5-inch/38-caliber gun mounts is a cable reel, for storing cables. On the side of the drum is a ring-gear and pinion assembly, for operating the reel with a hand crank (not installed).

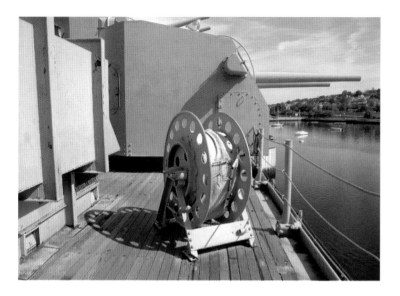

The cable reel shown in the preceding photo is viewed from another angle, facing forward on the superstructure deck. A canvas cover is lashed around the stored cable on the reel, to protect the cable from the elements. Numerous cable reels were on the decks.

The upper ammunition-handling room below 5-inch/38-caliber gun mount 5 is viewed, with the entry/exit door to the right. The structure is of welded construction. At the lower corner of the structure is a ventilator screen. To the left is the adjacent cable reel.

Blast bags, or bloomers, when present, were fastened to the rectangular frames mounted around the gunports. The curved hoops are bloomer protection rails, intended to keep the ample folds of the bloomers from becoming fouled in the gunports.

On the superstructure immediately above the top of the shield of 5-inch gun mount 5 are the foundation and tower for the starboard center Mk. 37 secondary-battery director. The round platform to the right of the gun mount supports a quad 40 mm Bofors antiaircraft gun mount.

The upper ammunition-handling room of 5-inch/38-caliber gun mount 5 is displayed, with the forward part of the ship to the right. The part of the structure in the foreground is a ventilator housing incorporated into the outboard side of the structure.

Just aft of 5-inch gun mount 5 is 5-inch gun mount 7. Like 5-inch gun mount 3, as well as gun mounts 4 and 8 on the port side of the superstructure deck, gun mount 7's stand rests directly on the deck, and its upper ammunition-handling room is one level below.

Inboard of 5-inch gun mount 7, mounted on the aft side of the ammunition-handling room of 5-inch gun mount 5, are four steel lockers that at least one source identifies as 20 mm ammunition lockers, but there were no 20 mm gun mounts in this immediate area.

The structure containing the upper ammunition-handling room for 5-inch/38-caliber gun mount 9 is viewed facing aft. On top of it is the ring-type stand for the gun mount, which contains the roller bearings upon which the mount rotates.

The aftermost 5-inch/38-caliber gun mount, number 9, is positioned above the structure containing the upper ammunition-handling room. To the left is the rear of 5-inch/38-caliber gun mount 7, and to the right are the boat crane and a boat.

A quad 40 mm gun mount and 5-inch/38-caliber gun mounts 7 and 9 are in the foreground in this view facing forward on the starboard side of the main deck, toward the rear of the superstructure. To the left is the kingpost of the boat crane, with part of the boom of the crane being visible between gun mount 9 and the mainmast. The lower part of the mainmast has diagonal braces on each side, and ladders running up the mast are faintly visible. Braces securing the upper extent of the foremast to the forward fire-control tower are also in view.

Massachusetts had several ship's bells; this one is on the starboard side of the superstructure deck aft of 5-inch gun mount 9. Shrapnel damage caused by an enemy 8-inch shell during the Battle of Casablanca on November 8, 1942, is indicated by the red paint.

Some of the features on the aft starboard side of the superstructure are displayed, including the smokestack (*right*), 5-inch/38-caliber gun mounts 7 and 9, and the boat crane located on level 2, one level above the superstructure deck. On the side of the superstructure one level down from the boat crane are ventilators; a ship's bell is hanging to the right of them. The pipes with flared tops running along the rear of the smokestack are steam-escape pipes. Inboard of the boat crane kingpost is the aft fire-control tower, on top of which is the aft Mk. 38 primary-battery director, nicknamed "Spot 2." A searchlight is mounted on a small platform with guardrails on the rear of the aft fire-control tower.

As observed from aside turret 3, facing forward, USS *Massachusetts'* masts and directors bristle with radar antennas. In addition to these, there were various radio antennas and IFF (identification friend or foe) antennas on the ship.

On the roof of 5-inch/38-caliber gun mount 10, toward the aft port terminus of the superstructure deck, is a blast hood over the mount captain's hatch, to protect him from concussion from the blasts of nearby guns when he was observing through the hatch.

Inside a gallery in the port side of the superstructure on level 2 is a twin 5-inch loading machine. This was an apparatus upon which 5-inch gun crews could hone their proficiency at loading the guns without being confined within the gun mounts.

The 5-inch guns of gun mount 8 are trained over Battleship Cove. Partially visible aft of and higher than that mount is gun mount 10. Protruding from the front of the shield is one of the bloomer protection rails, which kept the bloomers from getting snagged in the gunports.

Looking aft from the port side of the superstructure deck, with a 5-inch gun mount to the right, the aft Mk. 38 primary-battery director, "Spot 2," looms above the superstructure. On South Dakota–class battleships, different versions of the primary-battery directors were installed in the forward and aft positions: the forward director was the Mod. 2 and the aft one was the Mod. 3. Normally, the personnel assigned to a Mk. 38 director consisted of a spotter, rangefinder operator, standby rangefinder operator and talker, pointer, trainer, cross-leveler, and radio operator. In addition to a number of telescopes and a 26.5-foot stereoscopic rangefinder, the director was equipped with several successive types of radar; currently mounted on the aft Mk. 38 director is a Mk. 8 radar antenna.

The rear and roof of the shield of a 5-inch/38-caliber gun mount on the port side of the ship are displayed. The roof-hatch operating mechanism has been removed from the upper center rear of the shield. The spotlight on the roof is a modern addition.

The bracket to which the bottom of the roof-hatch operating mechanism was attached is still on the rear of the shield. The cutout in the bottom center of the blast hood provided clearance for the connection between the hatch-operating mechanism and the hatch.

The three hawser-stowage reels displayed in the preceding photograph are viewed from the superstructure deck, showing the brackets that secure them in an upright position. Two of the reels have protective canvas wrappings lashed in place around the cables, to protect them from moisture. The area is slightly forward of the smokestack; the two port steam-escape pipes on the rear of the stack are visible to the upper right. Above the two cable reels on the right, the vertical tube and slanting structure above it are part of the foundation for the port center Mk. 37 secondary-battery director, which is out of the view above the top of the photo.

Several hawser-stowage reels and their mounting brackets on the port side of the superstructure deck are viewed from above. To the right is a storage locker, and at the top of the photograph is the rear of a 5-inch/38-caliber gun mount.

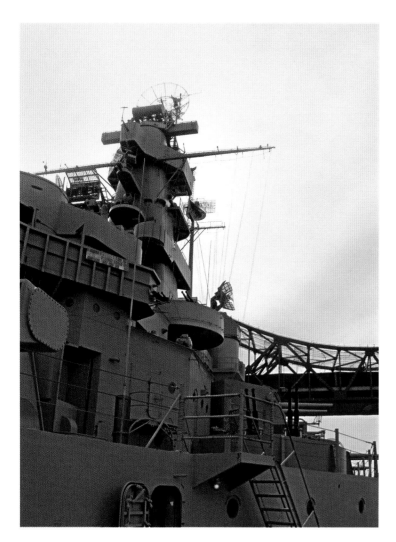

The quad 40 mm antiaircraft mount indicated in the preceding photo is viewed close up, facing aft. The trainer's and the pointer's control handwheels are present on the mount, as are the ring sights with their guards; 5-inch gun mount 2 is in the background.

The forward part of the superstructure is seen from the port side of the main deck. The door at the bottom leads into a corridor providing access to several wardroom staterooms, a fan room, and other compartments. Aft of the stairway landing at the center, on the superstructure deck, is a quad 40 mm antiaircraft gun mount mounted in a tub, just aft of which is 5-inch/38-caliber gun mount 2. To the upper left is the bridge, and above it is the top of the conning tower, on which one of the vision slots is visible. Rising above the superstructure is the forward fire-control tower, with the Mk. 38 Mod. 2 primary-battery director on top of it.

Mounted on the superstructure deck near the front of the superstructure is a whip antenna with an expanded-steel-mesh guard around its lower part. In the background are the left rear of turret 2 (*left*) and the front of the conning tower, behind the antenna.

A ventilator plenum is in the foreground of this image of the left side of turret 2, facing forward, with the left 16-inch gun of turret 1 visible in the distance. At the top center is the left hood of the rangefinder. A handrail is mounted under the top of the plenum.

The conning tower at the superstructure-deck level is viewed from a different angle than that shown in the preceding photograph. The prominent indentation in the conning tower is present on both sides of the structure. On this part of the conning tower, the armored structure is clad with a metal skin secured with rivets and welded seams. Also present on the tower are electrical lines and a wire-antenna fitting. Toward the top, the struts that help stabilize and strengthen the bridge are in view. Bracing strips also were applied to the side and bottom of the bridge.

From approximately the same vantage point as in the preceding photo, the rear of turret 2 is shown, including the platform with guardrails suspended under the gunhouse hatch and the handrails and footrails, which were retrofitted at some point.

The left hood of the rangefinder of turret 2 is viewed close up, showing the access plate screwed to the side of the hood and the viewing port on the front of the hood. The hood is attached to the gunhouse with hex screws. At the top right is the bridge.

The hoods for the left trainer's (upper) and pointer's telescopes protrude from the side of turret 2. There was a pointer and a trainer on each side of the gunhouse, and their duty was to lay the guns on the target when the mount was under local control.

The front port area of the superstructure is observed from the superstructure deck, with two guns of the quad 40 mm gun mount appearing in the foreground. The left wing of the bridge is at the upper left. At the center of the photo is a round platform and tub for another quad 40 mm Bofors antiaircraft gun mount; the gun barrels are peeking over the top of the tub. To the bottom right is the right side of 5-inch/38-caliber gun mount 2; directly above it is the port center Mk. 37 secondary-battery director, mounted on top of it a Mk. 12 radar antenna combined with a Mk. 22 "orange peel" radar antenna.

The port side of the bridge of USS *Massachusetts* is in view, including the enclosed section with square windows at the front of the bridge. A board with campaign ribbons is also present. A good view is provided of the system of struts underneath the bridge.

Underneath the bridge is a network of frame members that are continuations of the exposed braces on the sides of the bridge above. Also, underneath the bridge are exposed electrical cables for the navigational equipment located on the bridge.

Above the superstructure at the top right, the left side of the forward Mk. 37 secondary-battery director, "Sky 1," is visible. The box-shaped object near the top of that side is a cover where originally the cylindrical-shaped left side of the rangefinder protruded.

At the center of the photo, on the port side of the level atop the navigating bridge, known as the housetop, is a curved splinter shield. The raised enclosure at the rear of the curved splinter shield is a tub housing a Mk. 51 director. The starboard side is similar.

A covered motorboat is stowed on the starboard side of level 2, one level above the superstructure deck, alongside the rear of the smokestack. As World War II progressed, the number of boats carried on board the ship was reduced.

The motorboat is viewed from off its starboard bow. It rests on chocks, with outrigger braces to stabilize the boat. This method of stowing the boat saved on weight. Portions of the boat crane's boom and kingpost are visible aft of the boat.

A close-up shows details of the chocks and the outrigger braces for the motorboat. In the foreground, a stabilizer rod is connected to the brace in the foreground and to the chock's beam. To the left is the rear of 5-inch gun mount 9.

Massachusetts' boat is observed from aft, showing its single propeller and rudder. Visible above the boat and projecting from the side of the superstructure are two small antiaircraft gun-director tubs.

Most of the boat crane is visible in this view from off the starboard beam of the ship. The kingpost is adjacent to the rear of the aft fire-control tower, while the boom extends at an angle behind the 5-inch/38-caliber gun mount. Originally the ship had two cranes, but now only this crane remains. The crane rotated around the kingpost. The heel of the crane is attached to pivot points on a platform around the crane; this platform also holds the hoisting gear and cable drums. Other platforms around the kingpost were dedicated to the topping gear and reduction gear. The maximum elevated angle of the boom under a full load was 70 degrees from horizontal.

SPECIFICATIONS AND GENERAL DATA

Builder	Bethlehem Steel Company, Fore River Yard, Quincy, Massachusetts
Laid down	July 20, 1939
Launched	September 23, 1941
Commissioned	May 12, 1942
Length overall	680 ft., 0 in.
Length at waterline	666 ft., 0 in.
Maximum beam	107 ft., 11 in.
Waterline beam	108 ft., 2 in.
Mean draft	31 ft., 75/16 in. @ 42,329 tons
Maximum draft	34 ft., 9½ in. forward, 36 ft., ¾ in. aft
Displacement	35,113 tons light, 1946
	45,216 tons full load, 1946
Machinery	
Boilers	8 Babcock & Wilcox three-drum divided wall
Geared turbines	4 sets of General Electric double reduction, 185 rpm
Shaft horsepower	133,000 forward, 32,000 astern
Generators	7 ships service, 450 volt, 3 phase, 1,000 W
	2 emergency diesel, 450 volt, 3 phase, 200 kW
Speed	27.08 knots @ 185 rpm
Fuel oil capacity	1,952,208 gallons
Diesel fuel capacity	50,630 gallons
Aviation gasoline	9,130 gallons
Reserve feed water	12,000 gallons
Potable water	52,000 gallons
Complement 1945	2,339 (168 officers, 2,500 enlisted)
Cost	$76,885,750

The boat crane is observed from the forward end of the boom. The yellow hook hovering above the bow of the boat is the boat hook, which had a capacity of 27,000 pounds. The maximum extension of the boat hook from the center of the kingpost was a little over 52 feet. The crane and boom also accommodated a cargo whip, or cable, routed over the sheave at the very end of the boom, and attached to the end of the whip is the whip hook, seen at the bottom right. This hook was rated at 7,000 pounds. To the right is the rear of the smokestack, with the two starboard steam-escape pipes running along it.

The boat hook is mounted on a block, and the boom sheaves over which the boat hook cables pass on their way back to the hoist winch are mounted several feet back from the end of the boom. The sheave at the end of the boom accommodates the whip cable.

As viewed from the rear of the boat crane on level 2, the control platform (*top*) and hoisting-gear platform (*bottom*) surround the kingpost. Visible on the control platform is an array of handwheels for operating the crane. On the platform below it, there is a hydraulic motor on each side of the kingpost, to power the hoisting winches. The lower part of the kingpost extends below this level, where there are two more platforms with crane machinery, including topping machinery, which controlled the angle of the boom, and the reduction gear for the electrohydraulic power drive of the crane. Each of the topping, hoisting, and rotating gears had its own separate power source.

The hoisting-gear platform is viewed facing aft, showing the mounting points for the heel of the boom. The wide drum is for the boat-hook cable, while the narrow drum to the right is for the whip cable. To each side of the drums is a winch gearbox.

The boat crane is observed obliquely from the rear, showing the topping sheaves and cables that operated the boom. A ladder is attached to the rear of the kingpost. To the top left are the aft Mk. 38 primary-battery director and a platform with a 24-inch searchlight

A few steps starboard of the kingpost of the boat crane on level 2 is a railing with a view down to the ship's bell and the shrapnel damage from the November 1942 Battle of Casablanca. The steel deck below the bell is the superstructure deck.

Toward the aft end of level 2 are two side-by-side quad 40 mm gun mounts. The one in the foreground is the starboard mount, while the port mount is to the right. To the far left is the quad 40 mm gun mount atop turret 3. The aft Mk. 37 director is at the center.

Features on the aft portion of level 2 are observed from the starboard side, with the rear of turret 3 to the left. The quad 40 mm gun mount seen in the preceding photo is near the center of this photo, just forward of the aft Mk. 37 secondary-battery director.

The rear of the aft Mk. 37 secondary-battery director is observed on level 2. In the background, the Braga Memorial Bridge over the Taunton River poses a challenge to discerning the framework supporting the Mk. 12 and Mk. 22 radar antennas.

Directly below the housing of the aft Mk. 37 director is its ring-type stand, with exposed electrical conduits, cables, and boxes present on it. Some of the electrical components have been stripped, leaving exposed several brackets and mounting holes.

The Mk. 12 radar antenna atop the aft Mk. 37 secondary-battery director is viewed from the starboard side. The Mk. 12 was a 33 cm radar capable of automatically tracking the range of the target and calculating its range rate at ranges of up to 45,000 yards (25.6 miles).

As seen from the right rear quarter of the aft Mk. 37 director, the large antenna at the center is the Mk. 12, while the oblong, parabolic antenna to the right is the Mk. 22, which calculated the height of an approaching aircraft. It measures 1.5 by 6 feet.

Looming directly above the aft port quad 40 mm gun mount near the rear of level 2 is the tub for the director that controlled that mount. Visible above the top of the tub is a Mk. 57 director. This director, introduced late in the war, was equipped with a Mk. 34 radar.

In the foreground is the aft starboard quad 40 mm antiaircraft gun mount near the rear of the superstructure on level 2, showing the trainer's ring sight and control handwheel. The tub containing the director that controlled this quad 40 mm gun mount is at the top center. The view is facing forward, with the kingpost of the boat crane in the center background. Directly above the 40 mm gun barrels is the platform surrounding the kingpost that contained the controls for the boat crane. Below the director tub is a loudspeaker, and mounted on the side of the tub is a spotlight.

The forward ends of the tubs of the quad 40 mm gun mounts toward the rear of level 2 are open. This is the port mount. The stanchion in the foreground supports a gun director and tub above. At the upper center is the aft Mk. 37 secondary-battery director.

On the port side of level 2 adjacent to the rear of the superstructure is a 40 mm loading machine, an apparatus upon which 40 mm gun crews could practice their proficiency and speed in loading their weapons without having to do so on the actual weapons.

The 40 mm loading machine is viewed from the side. Crewmen loaded four-round clips of dummy ammunition into the replica of an automatic loader, the black fixture atop the device to the right. The machine is powered by electric motors driving flywheels.

As viewed from its rear, the 40 mm loading machine has two facsimiles of an automatic loader, the mechanized feed chute on top of a 40 mm Bofors gun's receiver. This feature of the loading machine mimics the arrangement of the actual 40 mm gun mount, where two guns are mounted together. Thus, two gun loaders can stand to each side of the loading machine and practice loading ammunition clips. On the right of the loading machine is the right flywheel, with a guard cage over it. The electric motor that drove this flywheel is mounted under the front end of the loading machine.

On level 2 between frames 93 and 97 is a gallery containing two 5-inch/38-caliber loading machines. Similar to the 40 mm loading machine, these fixtures enabled gun crews to practice loading their pieces, except out in the open air, unconfined to a gunhouse.

The two fixtures between the 5-inch loading machines are projectile hoists. In the actual 5-inch gun mounts, a projectile hoist was an apparatus that conveyed 5-inch projectiles by electrohydraulic power from the belowdecks ammunition-handling room up to the gunhouse.

The fixtures resembling a box with a drum to the rear atop the loading machines are the powered rammers, which rammed the projectiles and powder charges into the chamber. The boxy structure is the rammer tank, and the drum-shaped object is the rammer motor.

Level 3, the third level above the main deck, is the flag bridge. The view is to the port quarter. On the left is the flag bag, where the ship's signal flags were methodically stored. On the opposite side of level 3 is the starboard flag bag, similar in layout to this one.

The full extent of the curved bulwark shown in the preceding photo is shown, with the port flag bag to the extreme left. As can be seen, this curved bulwark, along with a corresponding curve in the deck, provided clearance for 5-inch gun mount 2.

Details of the bulwark and its framing on the port side of the flag bridge are visible. To the top left is the blast hood over the mount captain's hatch on 5-inch gun mount 2. In the background is a platform with guardrails for a 24-inch searchlight.

The 24-inch searchlight on the port side of the flag bridge is seen up close, showing the clear lens on its front. The lens is installed on a hinged, ring-shaped frame with a grab handle at the front, and the lens and frame are secured in place by clamp handles.

Tubular legs with diagonal braces support the platform for the 24-inch searchlight on the flag bridge. The door with a window in the background leads into the port side of the forward, enclosed portion of the flag bridge. To the upper right is the navigating bridge.

The 24-inch searchlight on the port side of the flag bridge is viewed from above, facing aft, showing the circular shape of the platform. Illumination of the searchlight was by carbon arc, and the searchlight was used primarily for signaling, with secondary uses for navigating and visual searching and detection. Atop the barrel of the light is a ventilating-fan housing. According to deck plans for USS *Massachusetts*, originally an admiral's chair was mounted on the deck just forward of the searchlight platform, to the bottom of the photo. The barrels of all five of the port 5-inch/38-caliber gun mounts are visible in this view, giving a sense of the tremendous firepower these weapons could bring to bear on enemy targets in the air or on the surface.

A view of the 24-inch searchlight on the port side of the flag bridge shows the ventilating-fan housing on top, to the right of which is an open sight and a bracket for a spotting telescope. Inside the lamp was an iris shutter for turning off the beam.

Near the door into the enclosed part of the starboard side of the flag bridge is an alidade mounted on a D-shaped platform. When the dome-shaped cover of the alidade was removed, it exposed a sighting device and azimuth scale, for establishing bearings.

A fine view is offered of the forward part of the main deck and turrets 1 and 2 from the forward starboard corner of the open-air portion of the flag bridge. The bulwark was designed with an outward curve at the top to deflect wind and water; several braces on the inner side of the bulwark are in view. To the far left is a portion of an alidade, an instrument that enabled the operator to take bearings on distant objects and landmarks. At the top left is part of the navigating bridge, showing some of the electrical wiring and framing underneath it.

The 24-inch searchlight on the starboard side of the flag bridge is observed facing forward. The round device aft of the grab handle on the frame of the lens is the signal-shutter operating motor. A handle would be installed on this motor to tap out signals.

The starboard 24-inch searchlight and platform on the flag bridge are viewed facing aft. The box-shaped assembly on the bottom of the drum of the searchlight is the lamp housing. The handles on the rear of the drum were for manually training and elevating the searchlight. The searchlight was of the automatic high-intensity carbon-arc type and had unlimited rotation and a range of elevation from 110 degrees to –30 degrees. To the upper right is the underside of the navigating-bridge deck, and the rounded platform and tub projecting above the searchlight is a quad 40 mm antiaircraft gun mount on the housetop: that is, the level above the navigating bridge.

Aft of the searchlight on the starboard side of the flag bridge, a view of the starboard center Mk. 37 secondary-battery director is available. Visible above the starboard flag bag at the bottom of the photo is the cylindrical foundation post for the director. The angled structure above that post is also part of the support for the director as well as the section of the housetop that the director is mounted on. A similar structural arrangement is also present on the port side for the center port Mk. 37 director. The deck with the guardrails to the lower right is the navigating-bridge deck. A glimpse of the upper part of the mainmast is at the top right.

From alongside the curve in the bulwark on the starboard side of the flag bridge designed to give clearance to 5-inch/38-caliber gun mount number 1, the angled braces and the stanchions that support the 40 mm gun mount on the housetop are in the foreground.

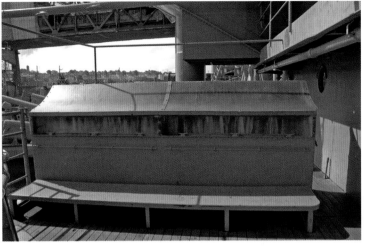

The starboard flag bag is on the flag bridge aft of the curved section of bulwark. To transmit signals by flags, flags stored in the flag bag would be run up halyards attached to yardarms extending from the upper part of the forward fire-control tower.

Naval Signal Flags

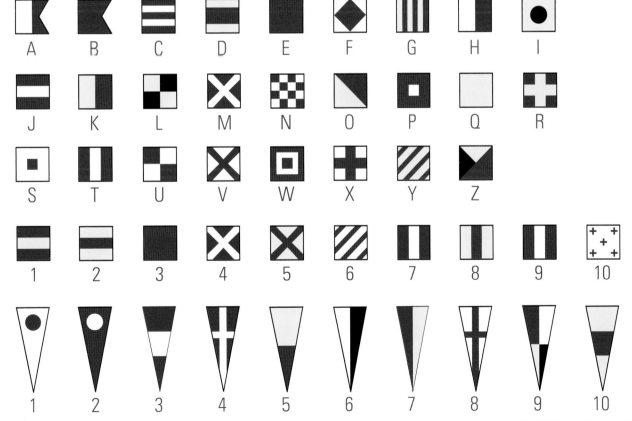

The bridge (*lower right*) originally was unenclosed, with a narrow walkway hugging the conning tower. In mid-1944 an enlarged but still-open bridge, with straight sides with vertical bracing, was installed. The current, enclosed, bridge dates to January 1946.

On the housetop, the level atop the navigating bridge, is a splinter shield (*center*) enclosing two Mk. 57 directors and, in raised tubs to the rear of the shield, two Mk. 51 directors. The tall object to the left of the splinter shield is a Mk. 27 radar antenna.

ARMOR SPECIFICATIONS

Main battery turrets	Face plates: 18.0 in.	
	Sides: 9.8 in.	
	Back: 12.0 in.	
	Roof: 7.25 in.	
Barbette armor	Centerline: 11.6 in.	
	Sides: 17.3 in.	
Secondary battery mounts	2.0 in. 78 lb. special-treatment steel (STS)	
Magazines	2.0 in.	
Conning tower armor, class B	Sides: 16.0	
	Beam: 16.0 in.	
	Roof: 7.25 in.	
	Communications tube: 16.0 in.	
Belt armor	12.2 in. class A on 0.875 in., 30 lb. STS, inclined 19 degrees	
Lower belt armor	12.2 in. class A on 0.875 in., 30 lb. STS, tapered to 1 in. on 0.75	
Deck armor	**Centerline**	**Outboard**
Main	1.5 in.	1.5 in.
Second	5.0 in. + 0.75 in.	5.3 in. + 0.75 in.
Third	0.3 in.	0.3 in.

The starboard side of the navigating bridge is viewed from the enclosed area at the front of the navigating bridge. In the foreground is the conning tower, including one of its vision slots, showing the great thickness of the armor on this structure.

An alidade located on the starboard side of the navigating bridge, visible in the background in the photo at left, is seen here up close. The dome-shaped cover of the alidade has been removed, exposing to view the azimuth scale housed in the top of the alidade.

The starboard side of the navigating bridge is viewed facing aft from the inboard side of the alidade (which is outside the view, to the left). Projecting from the housetop level is a quad 40 mm antiaircraft gun mount and guntub, below which are several 5-inch gun mounts.

From the same vantage point as in the preceding photo, a good view is available of the 24-inch searchlight and platform on the starboard side of the flag bridge. All five of the 5-inch/38-caliber gun mounts on the starboard side of the ship are visible.

In a view facing forward from the starboard side of the housetop, the starboard side of the navigating bridge is below to the right (note the alidade in the jog in the bulwark), the top of the conning tower is to the top left, and a gun-director tub is at the top center.

A view of from the port side of the housetop, facing forward, depicts the port side of the navigating bridge. The two small "boxes" on the rounded bulwark at the top are radio antenna trunks, where leads from wire antennas pass through insulators and into the ship.

Protruding through the top of the conning tower are five periscopes, which the personnel manning the tower relied on for visibility, since the tower's direct-vision fixtures were limited to a relatively few vision slots. The radar antenna is a nonoriginal fixture.

On the rear of the top of the conning tower is a Mk. 27 standby fire-control radar antenna (*left of center*) on a box-type mount. This radar system replaced the Mk. 40 stereoscopic rangefinder, which was originally located on top of the conning tower.

On the starboard side of the housetop aft of the conning tower (*right*) is a Mk. 57 director (*center*). Another Mk. 57 director is on the port side of this level. To the right is a raised tub for a Mk. 51 antiaircraft director, with ladder rungs providing access to it.

Nestled between the conning tower (*right*, with the Mk. 27 radar mount at the top) and tub for a Mk. 51 director (*left*) is the Mk. 57 director on the port side of the housetop. The radar antenna of the Mk. 57 director is on the front of the unit, facing toward shore.

The Mk. 51 director tub aft of the Mk. 57 director on the port side of the housetop is viewed. The top of the director is visible above the top of the tub, but the gunsight is not installed. Some of the original electrical boxes and controls are still on the tub.

On the front of the forward Mk. 37 director are hinged port covers for the telescopes of, *left to right*, the trainer, the pointer, and the control officer. Footrails and handrails are arranged around the housing to enable crewmen to access exterior components.

The forward Mk. 37 secondary-battery director, nicknamed "Sky 1," is viewed from behind, with the rear of the conning tower visible to the far right. On the right side of the director is the box-shaped protective housing installed over the right side of the Mk. 42 rangefinder at some point after the ship's 1945–46 refit: probably when the ship was being prepared for long-term storage with the Atlantic Reserve Fleet. A similar housing is over the left side of the rangefinder. On the rear of the cylindrical foundation of the director is a crew access door, above which is an outrigger, to which are attached wire antennas.

At the lower center is the housing over the left extension of the Mk. 42 rangefinder of the forward Mk. 37 director. A small vision port is in the front of the housing, apparently to permit checking the operation of the optics of the rangefinder. Mounted on the side of the director, to the front of the rangefinder housing, is a vertical ladder. To the top right, part of the Mk. 12 radar antenna is visible. In the background is the forward fire-control tower. Visible on the front of the tower just above the top of the Mk. 37 director is a 36-inch searchlight on a platform. The platform and bulwark surrounding the conning tower two levels above the searchlight are part of the forward air-defense station.

The right housing for the Mk. 42 rangefinder on the forward Mk. 37 director lacks the viewing port that is present on the left housing. Above that housing, to the side of the Mk. 12 radar antenna, is the Mk. 22 "orange peel" radar antenna. This radar unit enabled the Mk. 37 director to accurately gauge the height of an oncoming enemy aircraft, thus resulting in a much-improved firing solution than was possible before the Mk. 22 radar was added to the director. At the top of the forward fire-control tower is the Mk. 38 main-battery director, with the rangefinder housings extending from each side of the director. To the bottom right is the left side of the center starboard Mk. 37 director.

On each side of the housetop, just aft of the forward Mk. 37 director, is a platform and tub for a quad 40 mm antiaircraft gun mount. This one is on the port side. The tub is fitted with footrails and handrails, and two diagonal braces help support the structure.

The quad 40 mm gun mount on the port side of the housetop has been stripped of some of its components, including the ring sights and sight guards, as well as the ready-ammunition racks that originally lined the inside of the guntub.

The trainer's footrests are still present on the quad 40 mm gun mount on the port side of the housetop, but his seat and hand controls are missing. In the background is the center port Mk. 37 secondary-battery director and its cylinder-shaped foundation. Optical and radar information from this director and the other three Mk. 37 directors was routed to the plotting room belowdecks, where analog computers calculated firing solutions for the 5-inch/38-caliber guns. The Mk. 37 directors could also be used to control the 40 mm guns and, in emergency conditions, the 16-inch guns.

The quad 40 mm gun mount on the starboard side of the housetop is viewed facing aft. Components are also missing from this mount, including, as seen here, the pointer's ring sight, seat, and hand controls. The guardrail is also missing from the loaders' platform at the rear of the mount. Details are visible of the handrail and its mounting brackets around the upper exterior of the guntub. The starboard center Mk. 37 secondary-battery director is present in the background. The drum-shaped structure to the upper right is a Mk. 51 director tub; a similar one is on the opposite side of this level.

On each side of the aft end of the housetop level, adjacent to the smokestack, are two Mk. 51 directors in tubs. This one is on the starboard side, facing aft, with the tub of another Mk. 51 director partly visible to the left. Full-length openings in the tubs provided easy access to the director operator. The sight and several other components are no longer mounted on the director. The smokestack is to the right of the directors, just outside the photograph view. In the background to the lower right is part of the roof and the rear of the shield of 5-inch/38-caliber gun mount 9.

In a view from the starboard beam, the two Mk. 51 directors seen in the preceding photograph are next to the smokestack, just aft of the foundation of the center starboard Mk. 37 director. Many of the ship's radar and radio antennas are also displayed.

The smokestack is viewed looking upward from the starboard side. The tubs of the two Mk. 51 directors indicated in the preceding photos are in the foreground. At the top of the stack is the funnel cap, painted matte black; whip antenna supports are on its side.

The foremast (*left*) and mainmast (*right*) are portrayed in this view of the smokestack from the port quarter. A Mk. 51 director and tub were mounted directly to each side of the smokestack in a July 1944 refit, but these were removed during a 1946 refit.

The port side of the flag bridge is viewed from alongside the smokestack, facing aft, with the angled struts of the mainmast and the aft Mk. 38 main-battery director appearing in the left background. There is no corresponding section of flag bridge on the starboard side, in order to provide clearance for the boat crane. As built, there was a boat crane and boat stowage in the area depicted in this view, but these were eliminated during a refit in World War II. During the war, there was a gallery of five 20 mm Oerlikon antiaircraft gun mounts along this part of the flag bridge.

The aft part of the superstructure is viewed from the starboard side, with the smokestack positioned between the mainmast and the foremast. The kingpost of the boat boom is toward the left, to the upper left of which is the aft Mk. 38 main-battery director.

In a view looking forward from the aft port part of the flag bridge, the mainmast and its struts are in the foreground. The two Mk. 51 director tubs at the aft port corner of the housetop level in the background have been touched up with red primer. Just beyond these two tubs is the center port Mk. 37 secondary-battery director, pointing outboard. Outriggers jut from the mainmast at the level of the funnel cap, and the outriggers are stiffened by diagonal braces. A small searchlight is mounted on a stanchion adjacent to the port brace of the outriggers.

The funnel cap, whip antenna mounts, foremast, and, *to the right*, the center starboard Mk. 37 director are observed. The large dish antenna on the foremast at the center is the SK-3, above which on the top foremast is an SG-1b surface-search radar antenna.

Radar antennas on the mainmast (*left*) and foremast are seen from the aft starboard quarter. SG-1b surface-search radar antennas are near the tops of both masts. The large, rectangular antenna on the maintop is the SR-A secondary air-search radar.

The aft Mk. 38 main-battery director, "Spot 2," is observed from near the aft port quarter of the smokestack (*far left*), facing aft. This director is equipped with a Mk. 8 fire-control radar antenna on top, whereas the forward Mk. 38 director has the Mk. 18 radar.

Another view of the aft Mk. 38 main-battery director shows it from the starboard side. The director is mounted on a funnel-shaped tower, with a searchlight platform (partially obscured by the kingpost of the boat crane) partway up its aft facet. The director on top of the tower rotated to track enemy surface and land targets. The 26.5-foot stereoscopic rangefinder protruding from each side of the director provided optical range information, while the 10 cm Mk. 8 fire-control radar could quickly fix the range of an enemy target. The polyrods protruding from the front of this antenna gave this antenna its nickname, the comb antenna.

The rotating part of the Mk. 38 director is above the searchlight. At the outer ends, hinged covers protect the openings for the rangefinder objectives. On the front of the center part of the director are hinged covers for the trainer's and pointer's telescopes.

The front of the Mk. 8 fire-control antenna atop the aft Mk. 38 main-battery director is displayed. This radar was manufactured by Western Electric and is considered the first track-while-scanning radar. It featured a wide field of view and could pinpoint the range of a capital ship at 40,000 yards (22.7 miles) or a submarine at 10,000 yards (5.7 miles). While the Mk. 8 radar on the forward Mk. 38 director was replaced by the Mk. 15 radar during a 1945–46 refit, the Mk. 8 radar remained on the aft Mk. 38 director. Below the Mk. 8 radar antenna is the searchlight mounted on the aft facet of the aft fire-control tower.

A Mk. 57 director equipped with radar is mounted in a tub to the rear of the aft fire-control tower. The radar antenna is to the right of the director's pedestal. Below are turret 3 and the aft part of the main deck. To the bottom left is a quad 40 mm gun mount.

Surrounded by the steel of *Massachusetts'* hull and superstructure was a floating city—home to thousands of men. This required the facilities of a small town, including a jail, or brig in Navy parlance. This was used to confine enlisted men who committed serious offenses such as assault and battery, theft, dereliction of duty, etc. Officers found to commit such offenses were typically confined to quarters.

Counter to the brig, the gedunk, or soda fountain, offered sailors a respite from the heat. *Massachusetts*, like most large US combatant ships, was equipped to produce her own ice cream, which was not only a treat for her crew but a valuable trading commodity for needed items obtained from less well-equipped ships.

Aboard *Massachusetts* was a complete printshop, used to create official notices as well as printing the ship's newspaper, the Bay Stater. At far right is the Linotype machine, which was used to cast the lead type, which was then assembled into a printing plate, which in turn was used by the Kluge printing press (*at left*) to actually print the documents.

Various sizes of paper were required, depending on the print job. This Craftsman Chandler & Price paper cutter was used to cut large stacks of paper to size. In the left foreground is the imposing stone, a stone-surfaced table upon which pages or columns of type were assembled, or framed, before being placed in the press.

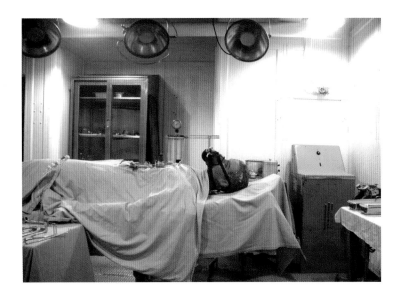

Massachusetts had a fully equipped operating room, for performing surgeries on battle casualties or on crewmen who were injured or suffering from maladies. The operating room also had x-ray equipment.

This is one of several battle-dressing (first aid) stations spread about *Massachusetts*. These were used to treat men during the height of battle, when because of the closing off of watertight compartments it may have been difficult to get a patient to sick bay.

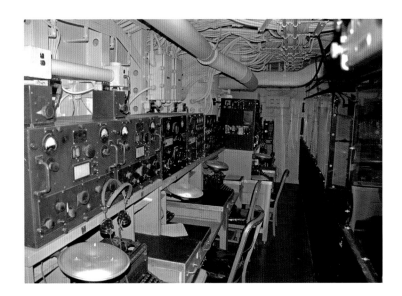

Radio central, on the third deck, is the place where operators sat at their sets, day and night, sending signals and receiving and typing transcripts of messages and orders from the fleet commands.

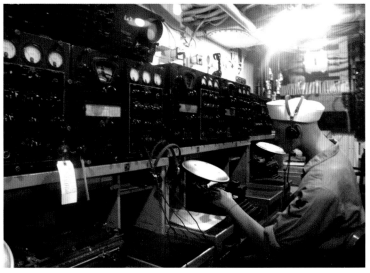

Radio Central was the main radio station of USS *Massachusetts*. All messages were then decoded. Transcribing of messages was done on manual typewriters. Transcripts of coded messages were then sent to the decoding room.

This is the pay office aboard *Massachusetts*. During *Massachusetts'* time in use, much of the payroll to the men of the ship was made in cash, and upon occasion the small safe in this office held $1 million in currency.

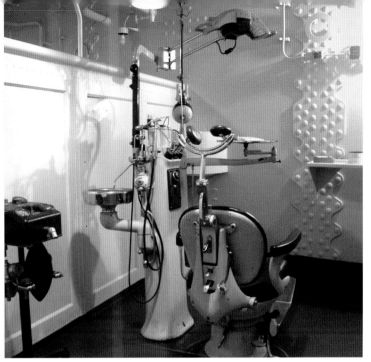

As with physician's spaces, *Massachusetts* was equipped with dental facilities and a dental staff to attend both to the routine dental needs of the crew as well as dental problems brought about by injury. It was not uncommon for men from lesser-equipped ships to be brought aboard for treatment.

A portion of the extensive machine shop aboard *Massachusetts*, with an end mill (*foreground*) and three lathes visible. Ships at sea did not have the luxury of turning to shipyard warehouses for replacement parts; rather, components had to be repaired, or replacements fabricated, in this shop.

Some parts were impractical to make at sea, such as lightbulbs and other electrical components. Thus, storerooms held replacement parts, as here. Lightbulbs were a high-casualty item, since the pounding from firing the 16-inch battery caused many bulbs to fail.

Feeding the hardworking men of *Massachusetts* was a formidable task, as evidenced by the massive size of this dough mixer (*left*). The placard on the wall above the mixer indicates that a batch of biscuits required 200 pounds of flour, 16 pounds of sugar, 48 pounds of shortening, and various other ingredients.

Baking in such quantities required this arsenal of ovens. Just beyond the ovens are a number of cooling or proofing racks.

Massachusetts had large, refrigerated compartments, which allowed her to take aboard large cuts of meat, which this butcher shop then cut to the appropriate size for the meals her cooks were preparing. This sometimes even included steak.

Vegetables and produce were stored in this "spud locker," which is equipped with an industrial potato peeler (the cylindrical gray object, *at center*) and a potato slicer (to the left of the peeler).

The main galley is where most of the cooking for the ship's company was done. It is on deck 2 and abuts the barbette of turret 3, which is visible behind the soup kettles. Also in view are sinks, food preparation tables, ventilation trunks, and exposed plumbing.

Typically, the crew was served cafeteria style through this serving line. During long periods of general quarters, the cooks would prepare trays of sandwiches that were taken to the men at their battle stations.

In addition to the ovens used by the bakers, the main galley had its own assortment of ovens for use when preparing meals.

The ongoing addition of antiaircraft armament and electronics meant that the size of *Massachusetts'* crew increased considerably beyond that called for in her initial design. Accordingly, crew quarters were crammed into every available space, as evidenced by these bunks hanging by chain from the overhead.

In the right foreground is the forward of two master gyrocompasses, with the auxiliary conning station in the center background. The master gyrocompass supplied the ship's true compass heading to repeater compasses at numerous other stations around the ship.

Firing solutions were calculated by Mk. 8 range keepers, which were analog computers, one of which is shown to the right. Each computer operated together with a stable element, an instrument that corrected for the pitch and roll of the ship, one of which is in the left foreground. In the background is an electrical switchboard. The red floor panels were removable.

The stable element is a vertical-seeking gyroscope that accounts for the rolling or pitching of the ship when aiming the guns. In the event the ship suddenly changes course, a signal from the master gyrocompass momentarily disables the action of this device, so as to prevent it from losing true vertical. Three brass hand-firing keys are visible on the face of the stable element. The leftmost key causes an alarm to sound, alerting that firing is about to commence. The center key activates the firing circuit, pending the gyroscope output confirming the roll or pitch, to bring the guns to bear. The far-right key is an emergency-firing key, which bypasses everything else to fire the gun or guns that have been selected.

This is the powder-handling floor of one of *Massachusetts*' 16-inch/45-caliber turrets. On the circular bulkhead, to the right of center, two of the six powder-passing scuttles are visible. These provided a safe means of transferring powder bags from the magazine, outside the turret, into the powder-handling floor. From these scuttles, powder handlers carried the powder charges to the powder hoists, one of which is seen at center. The hoists rotated in unison with the turret.

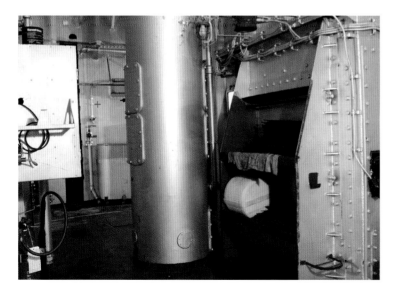

There were three powder hoists for each turret, serving the three guns in the turret. The hoists were arranged in two groups: a single one and a double one. Six powder bags constituted one powder charge for a gun, with the hoist capable of lifting three bags at once. This hoist has one bag in it. To the left is the central column of the turret.

This photo taken aboard USS *Iowa* in 1986 illustrates how shells were moved from their storage places on the projectile flat by means of a procedure called parbuckling, whereby a motorized "gypsy head" capstan (*center*) operated a line routed around a pulley and the lower part of the projectile. In the case shown here, the projectile is being skidded from its storage spot on the outer ring to the inner ring, which rotated in either direction to bring the projectile as close as possible to a projectile hoist. There were six gypsy heads on each projectile flat. Projectiles were secured by large roller chains known as projectile lashings. *Massachusetts* used an identical procedure and has a nearly identical layout of this area. *US Navy*

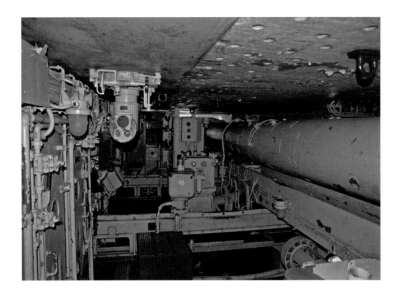

At the rear of each 16-inch gunhouse is the turret officer's booth; the view faces the right side. To the right is the rangefinder, and a yellow periscope is to the left. Rammers for the guns are on the floor. The gun chambers are on the other side of the bulkhead, *to the left*.

Powder for the 5-inch/38-caliber dual-purpose weapons was stored in weatherproof metal cannisters in magazines belowdecks. The shell was separate from the charge and was also stored in magazines.

Each of the ten 5-inch/38-caliber gun mounts has a corresponding powder-handling room belowdecks, where powder charges for the guns are brought in from magazines and sent up hoists to the gun mounts. Shown here are two hoists with their doors open.

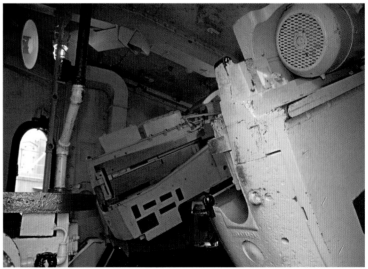

Inside the gunhouse of a 5-inch/38-caliber gun mount, the rear of the right gun is to the right, and the rear of the left gun is to the center. The left crew door is open to the left. At the top right is the rammer motor. In the background is a ventilator duct.

The ship's eight Babcock & Wilcox boilers produced steam that powered four sets of General Electric geared turbines. The General Electric double-reduction gears, the housing for one of which is shown here, converted the turbine rpm to rpm suitable for the propellers.

One of the Babcock & Wilcox three-drum express boilers is displayed. It is a twin-furnace design with a working pressure of 578 psi and temperature of 850 degrees Fahrenheit. To conserve space, designers of the South Dakota–class battleships grouped the boilers in the engine rooms with the turbines and reduction gears.

The engine room power was transmitted to the water via these four massive propellers. The five-bladed outboard props are 17 feet, 4 ½ inches in diameter, while the inboard three-bladed props measure 17 feet, 8 inches. Two semibalanced rudders guided the ship. *Moe Knox via Battleship Cove*

Today, USS *Massachusetts* forms the centerpiece of Battleship Cove, in Fall River, Massachusetts. Her big guns, long silent, provide mute testament to a bygone day of naval warfare. Inner spaces that were once the home to thousands of fighting men now form a memorial to those men, and hundreds of thousands more like them, who manned vessels like these, protecting the shores of the United States and fighting for justice around the globe. *Battleship Cove*